the Desert Home

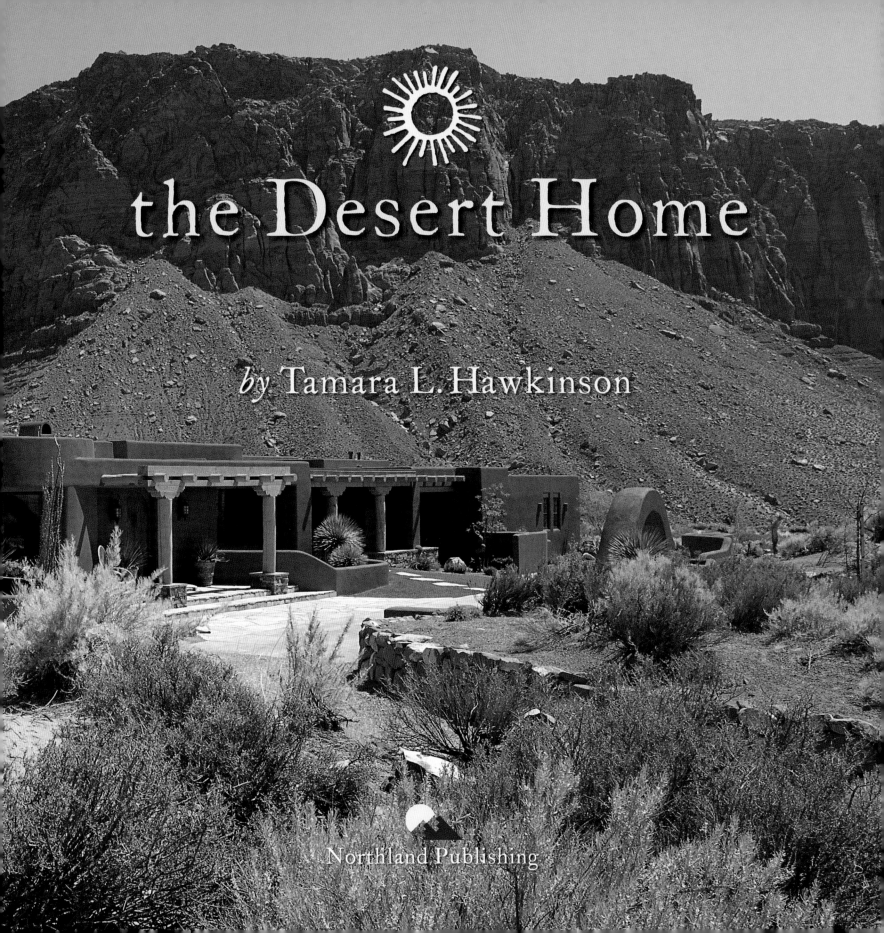

the Desert Home

by Tamara L. Hawkinson

Northland Publishing

www.northlandpub.com

Composed in the United States of America
Printed in Hong Kong

Edited by Tammy Gales
Designed by Jennifer Schaber
Production supervised by Donna Boyd

Photography © 2002 by:

Russell Bamert: 18, 21
Kirk Gittings: 19, 20
Brian Griffin: 100-105
Pedro E. Guerrero: 48 (bottom)
Klaus Kranz: 5 (top), 13, 35, 135
Terrence Moore: viii, 2, 8 (top), 14 (bottom), 22, 23, 30
    (bottom), 30-31 (background), 49 (top left, top right,
    bottom), 66-67, 76-77, 79, 81 (top), 84-93, 106 (top),
    106-107 (background), 107 (left), 116-118, 121
    (right), 122-133, 136, 139 (bottom), 140, 141
    (left & right), 148, 148-149 (background), 149
    (bottom right), 156-157 (background), 157
Bill Timmerman: front cover, 68-75, 107 (right)
Thomas Veneklasen: 38-47
Scott Zimmerman: ii-iii, 80, 94-99, 108-115, 137, 138

Courtesy Arizona Office of Tourism: 33, 34, 83 (left)
Courtesy Brian Lebel's Cody Old West Auction: 119
Courtesy CCBG Architects, Inc.: 9
Courtesy CCBG Architects, Inc., Photography by Jeffrey
    Green: 10-11
Courtesy CCBG Architects, Inc., Photography by Peter
    Malinowski: 139 (top)
Courtesy CCBG Architects, Inc., Photography by Scott
    Sandler: 1
Courtesy Cibolo Creek Ranch, Photography by Michael
    Wilson: 24-29
Courtesy El Paso County Historical Society: 4, 5 (bottom
    left, bottom center, bottom right), 17
Courtesy Est Est, Inc., Photography by Lydia Cutter: 64
Courtesy Est Est, Inc., Photography by Tony Hernandez:
    ii, x, 6, 30 (top), 31 (left & right), 50-63, 65

Courtesy Est Est, Inc., Photography by Dino Tonn: 106
    (bottom), 134, back cover
Courtesy Est Est, Inc., Photography by Ralph Rippe:
    v-vii
Courtesy Greater Phoenix Convention and Visitors
    Bureau: 8 (bottom right), 32, 36, 37
Courtesy Hurd-LaRinconada Gallery, Photography by
    Jan Butchofsky-Houser: 48-49 (background)
Courtesy Las Vegas News Bureau: 82, 83 (right)
Courtesy New Mexico Department of Tourism: 3, 12, 14
    (top), 15, 16, 78, 120
Courtesy Southwest Studies: 34, 81 (bottom)
Courtesy Ten Eyck: 156 (top & bottom), 158-159
Courtesy Ten Eyck, Photography by Richard Maack:
    150-155
Courtesy Ten Eyck, Photography by Alan McCoy:
    142-147, 149 (top)
Courtesy University Communications Office UTEP: 8
    (bottom left)
Courtesy Ventana del Valles, Photography by Russell Bamert:
    121 (left)
Courtesy Ventana del Valles, Photography by Lisa
    Mandelkern: 149 (bottom left)

FIRST IMPRESSION 2002
ISBN 0-87358-796-0

06 05 04 03 02   5 4 3 2 1

Library of Congress Cataloging-in-Publication Data

Hawkinson, Tamara L. (Tamara Logsdon)
        The desert home / by Tamara L. Hawkinson.
        p. cm.
        Includes bibliographical references and index.
        1. Architecture, Domestic—Southwestern States.
        I. Title.

        NA7224.6 .H38 2002
        728'.37'0979—dc21   2002067798

To My Grandmothers,
Mattie Marsalas Logsdon
and
Vilena Krumme Landers,
whose legacy continues to inspire me
each and every day.

Contents

Homes of the Desert Regions

Western Lifestyles & Influences

Preface

I HAVE BEEN A DESERT DWELLER for almost a decade now having made the conscious decision to leave the rolling green hills and high humidity of the Midwest for this land of cloudless skies and fiery sunsets. As an interior designer turned writer, I've trekked across this part of the country for the last several years, penning a couple travel guides and countless magazine articles on the West's fascinating history, and slipping in a few design articles as well.

So it was with a great amount of enthusiasm that I took on this project with Northland Publishing—a book on architecture and interior design. But soon I was faced with the daunting task of how to bring the unique lifestyle of America's desert communities into an organized format.

When you mention the Southwest, visions of Santa Fe usually come to mind. Mention desert cities—like Phoenix or Tucson—and you might envision a saguaro cactus or two, but it's harder to visualize a "look" beyond whitewashed furniture and the overused Kokopelli. As I began the odyssey of fleshing out just the right homes, I started categorizing the houses by style such as traditional, contemporary, etc. But as I continued to research the history and terrain of America's different deserts, it became apparent that this book should be segmented by desert, because it is those distinctive characteristics of each desert region that often define the styles we see today. The old adobe dwellings of Mesilla, New Mexico are vastly different from the homes of Palm Springs, California.

The United States has four desert regions, but this book focuses on only three—the Southwest's hot deserts: the Chihuahuan, Sonoran, and Mojave.

The fourth American desert, the Great Basin, is a cold desert, encompassing much of northern Nevada, and parts of Utah, Idaho, and Oregon.

The Chihuahuan Desert stretches from west Texas through southern New Mexico and into southeastern Arizona, but most of it is in Mexico. The Sonoran Desert includes the southern half of Arizona west to south-central California and south into Mexico. The Mojave Desert starts north of the Sonoran Desert in California and runs through a portion of southern Nevada and a small area in southwestern Utah.

These deserts have been inhabited for thousands of years with each new wave of emigrants adapting their native culture to the environment. What we have today is a blend of three predominant cultures: Native American, Spanish, and Anglo-American. All three have left their undeniable imprint from their language and customs to their crafts and foods, and especially, and most visibly in their architecture.

What you'll find in this book is a blend of the old styles and the new, from rural to urban, from mansion to cottage, with a special emphasis on outdoor living—a big part of the desert lifestyle. You'll also find profiles of several couples committed to "tread lightly" within the desert ecosystem. Their alternative homes are surely the wave of the future even though their environmental philosophies incorporate much from the past.

So come join us on this journey through America's desert Southwest, and you'll see what we desert dwellers have already discovered—the colorful landscape, the remarkable sunsets, the blend of cultures—all reasons we call the desert home.

PREVIOUS PAGE: **An inviting transition from the family room, this covered outdoor living area is sheltered from the sun but open to exquisite desert views.** OPPOSITE: **The desert sun casts a series of dramatic shadows in the sheltered outdoor living area of this Mojave desert home.**

The Desert Home

THE DESERT IS A STAGE of light and shadows, contrasting rugged textures, and vivid colors. Desert architecture and design reflect this landscape and its history. Today, desert homes are a blend of old and new, a blend of regional styles mixed with modern technology, and a blend of cultures. The unspoken mystique of the land; the sharp, bold shapes of the desert and its plants; the haunting and stark vistas; the blazing blue skies and electric sunsets; the gentleness of hand-formed adobe; the intense colors of Mexican design or soft hues of a Navajo rug—all are defining details in the homes of the desert Southwest.

The Three Deserts

North America's three hot deserts—the Chihuahuan, the Sonoran, and the Mojave—are uniquely diverse in geologic landforms, flora and fauna, and human histories. The richness of the terrain, the stark yet colorful landscapes, and the remarkable sunsets are all visions that typify the three desert areas of the Southwest.

The Chihuahuan Desert is the largest desert in North America, covering more than 200,000 square miles mostly in Mexico but including areas in Texas and New Mexico. Prickly-pear, yucca, agave, and

OPPOSITE: **Views at dusk of an expansive contemporary adobe dwelling perched in the desert foothills overlooking Phoenix, Arizona.** RIGHT: **This eclectic Monterey-style inspired home sits on the edge of a desert golf course. From the second story balcony, bedrooms and sitting rooms offer dramatic sunset views.**

creosote bush dot the rugged region, and lush vegetation snakes alongside the waters of the Rio Grande. Some of the most scenic desert landscape is found in Big Bend National Park in Texas and White Sands National Monument in New Mexico.

The Sonoran Desert, which spans 120,000 square miles across southern Arizona and into California, offers one of the most identifiable icons of the Southwest, the saguaro cactus. This desert is also home to the sand dunes in southwestern Arizona as well as the once-raging Colorado River, which winds its way south forming the Arizona/California border. Saguaro National Park and Organ Pipe Cactus National Park in Arizona and Anza-Borrego Desert State Park in California showcase this rich desert habitat.

The Mojave Desert is a sparsely populated 25,000 square mile area of California, Nevada, and Utah, encompassing the lowest spot in the nation and often the hottest. Many Americans first experienced this harsh terrain as they motored west in the 1930s along historic Route 66. Based on pronunciation discrepancies, two different spellings occur with *Mojave* more prevalent in California and *Mohave* in Arizona. Death Valley National Park, Joshua Tree National Park, and Mojave National Preserve in California highlight the region's flora and fauna.

Although each region has its own unique characteristics, the three deserts also share many features. Rainfall averages less than 10 inches per year. During the summer monsoon season, torrents of water fill parched creekbeds and dry washes, often causing the legendary desert flash flood, and skies glow with lightning. A single summer storm can spawn hundreds of strikes. And while a dusting

OPPOSITE TOP: The Sonoran Desert's rugged terrain is dotted with saguaro cactus, found nowhere else in the world. OPPOSITE BOTTOM: Sunset casts a purple hue over the Mojave Desert's sparsely vegetated mountain and basin topography. ABOVE: On the northern edge of the Chihuahuan Desert, the Gila Wilderness in New Mexico was the world's first designated wilderness area.

of snow in the high desert elevations quickly disappears once the sun emerges, some mountains remain snow-capped through the winter months.

Even the harshest desert terrain is teeming with life—from the prehistoric-looking Gila monster to delicate hummingbirds, from big-horned sheep to soaring hawks. Plant life is just as diverse with lush trees crowding along riparian areas, often a backdrop to the spiny, odd-shaped cactus. It is the cactus that truly defines the desert landscape, and surprisingly, these harsh thorny plants sprout delicate blossoms of intense hues each spring. In fact, during springtime, wildflowers and cactus flowers transform the desert into a patchwork of hot pink, deep coral, red, yellow, and orange.

But while the dramatic landscape and unusual flora and fauna certainly define these great deserts, it is the human history—the people and their culture—that gives the Southwest its greatest distinction.

The Three Cultures

Native American, Spanish, and Anglo-American— you'll see evidence of all three cultures as they blend across the Southwest—signage in Spanish and English, Native American arts and crafts, old Catholic missions, adobe homes, and prehistoric cliff dwellings.

The Indian Period, which is the region's first significant cultural influence, dates back to some-time around A.D. 300 as the Hohokam, Mogollon, and Anasazi developed throughout the Southwest. These prehistoric native peoples left an enduring impression with the remnants of their dwellings, offering a glimpse into their lifestyle. This is the only part of the United States where permanent indigenous architecture exists.

At first, the shelters were basic pits dug into the ground simply covered with brush. Eventually, buildings were constructed above ground out of the earth, and layers of mud formed the walls. Logs, sticks, and brush formed a flat roof where more layers of mud completed the structure. By the mid-1500s, the mud dwellings were engineered into structures four and five stories high. Some of these buildings have withstood time and can still be seen scattered throughout the Southwest region.

The Hispanic Period began when Spanish explorers ventured into the Southwest as early as 1539. A year later, Coronado was en route on his legendary expedition. By the spring of 1542, when he and his ragged army headed back into Mexico, the explorers had covered Arizona, New Mexico, parts of Texas, Oklahoma, and traveled as far north as Kansas. They visited the pueblos along the Rio Grande, entered the mouth of the Colorado River, and experienced the raw beauty of the Grand Canyon. But his quest was to discover cities filled with gold, silver, and jewels, and without that dis-covery, Coronado's expedition was considered a colossal failure.

It took another fifty years before any of the New World was colonized. In 1598, Don Juan de Ornate claimed possession of New Mexico for the Spanish crown. Franciscans were dispatched to promote Catholicism, inspiring a string of missions to be built over the next two hundred years throughout the Southwest.

The Spanish soon taught the Native Americans to make adobe bricks, a technique derived from North Africa. The bricks—a sun-dried mixture of

RIGHT: Montezuma's Castle, named by U.S. Army scouts after its discovery in the 1860s, is an example of the desert Southwest's indigenous architecture. Built around A.D. 1100, the five-story cliff dwelling is wedged high into an alcove and was occupied for over 300 years. OPPOSITE BOTTOM: After the 1680 Santa Fe revolt, the Tigua Indians fled south and established the Ysleta Mission near El Paso, making it the oldest Spanish mission in Texas. BOTTOM LEFT: Around 1682, the Socorro Mission was built in the same region. The original building was destroyed in a flood and rebuilt in 1843. BOTTOM CENTER: The San Elizario Presidio was founded to protect the river settlements of Ysleta and Socorro. BOTTOM RIGHT: Although all the missions were originally in Mexico, the gradual shifting of the Rio Grande, which was the official border between Mexico and the United States, eventually made them part of Texas. The Guadalupe Mission, dating from the 1600s, is just across the border in Juarez, Mexico.

clay, sand, water, and straw—replaced the "pud-dled" mud dwellings. Iron tools such as the ax, along with nails and other metals were also introduced by the Europeans. Exposed ceiling logs were transformed into square shapes, and ornate corbels, basic cabinetry, and hand-carved furniture were crafted. The Spanish added stone rubble footings to protect the adobe walls from the ground, and hinges, latches, and other hardware were all hand-forged.

By the end of the 18th century, the simple adobe brick buildings, and especially the missions, were adorned with festive carvings and brightly painted ornamentation. But by this time, the Spanish were loosing interest in the New World. Finally, in 1821, Mexico demanded their freedom and won their independence.

The American Period began soon thereafter, as stories of gold and silver strikes were making their way back East, luring thousands of pioneers to set out on the hazardous three-month trek in search of their fortune in California. It didn't take long for the United States government to recognize the value of these unoccupied western lands.

By 1846, the U.S. controlled the land all the way to the West coast, with the exception of a small area below the Gila River in New Mexico and Arizona. In 1853, the desire to connect the East and West through a southern railway spurred the U.S. to buy this parcel of land as well. With the Gadsden Purchase complete, the borders of the Lower Forty-eight as we know them today were finalized.

The Four Historic Building Eras

Just as the different deserts and various cultures have played a role in shaping the Southwest, so have the prevailing building styles. Today, the Southwest is a unique mix of the past and the future.

The Colonial Era dwellings built by those first Spanish explorers didn't change much over the first couple hundred years. These humble adobe structures were typically built contiguously around a central plaza in a fort-like configuration. Details included exposed ceiling beams—*vigas*—and smaller poles laid in a pattern over the vigas—*latillas*. Small windows pierced the thick adobe walls and the floors were made of compacted dirt.

By the 1830s, Americans, streaming into California at a steady pace, put a New England spin on adobe construction. The resulting two-story whitewashed adobe with pitched roof and overhanging balcony—dubbed "Monterey Style" after the city where it originated—is more prevalent in California than the typical flat-roofed adobe.

The Romantic Era began in the 1840s with the influx of easterners following the California gold rush. As the railroads punched through to the western shores, wood, glass, bricks, and other sophisticated building materials became readily available. As fortunes in these new lands were created, residents tossed out the local building styles and brought back the romantic styles that had been popular back East.

The Victorian Era began to flourish in southwestern cities when the regional fighting was finally over in the 1880s. Residences became less fort-like and for the most part, they abandoned the use of earthen materials. Relatively young

OPPOSITE: **Blending architectural elements from historical southwestern styles, this comfortable living area features a softly rounded, curving stairway, hand carved balusters, richly stained *vigas,* along with colorful weavings, custom furnishings, and accessories collected from around the region.**

cities, like El Paso and Phoenix, were fertile ground for new trends, and the era of elaborate homes was in full swing. Nothing was spared from this overdone style. Even Santa Fe's historic Palace of the Governors built in 1609 was "modernized" with Victorian details.

The Eclectic Era finally took hold around the turn of the century, as a host of styles prevailed. In the 1920s, a Spanish renaissance swept the nation. More popular in the West, stylized versions of historic designs were dubbed Pueblo Revival, Spanish Eclectic, Spanish Colonial Revival, and Territorial. By the middle of the 20th century, Frank Lloyd Wright and other contemporary architects were promoting the use of local earthen materials combined with simple lines and wide expanses of glass to take in the desert views.

Today, with the variety of building styles available, many desert dwellers are looking to lessons from the region's earlier inhabitants. Life was harsh and materials scarce—designs had to be practical. Earth architecture combined with passive solar techniques and new building technology has brought desert construction back to its roots.

OPPOSITE TOP: **Spanish colonial artifacts fill the courtyard of this Territorial-style adobe that dates from the mid-1800s in Mesilla, New Mexico.**
OPPOSITE BOTTOM LEFT: **The University of Texas at El Paso's President now resides in the renovated Hoover house built in 1917. The estate, gardens, and grounds extend a full block and are a popular** setting for community events. OPPOSITE BOTTOM RIGHT: **In an unlikely blend of Victorian style and desert terrain, a wealthy Phoenix, Arizona doctor built this elaborate home in 1895.** ABOVE: **Using strong, clean lines reminiscent of Frank Lloyd Wright's prairie style, the sprawling home overlooks a sea of city lights.**

Homes of the
Desert Regions

The Chihuahuan Desert

Although the Chihuahuan Desert is the largest desert in North America, it is probably the least known. The region, which encompasses parts of southeastern Arizona, southern New Mexico, and west Texas, stretches south almost to Mexico City—1200 miles long and 800 miles wide. In this "high desert" the rain is sparse, the summers hot, and the winters unusually cold. Unlike the neighboring Sonoran Desert, home to large cacti and small trees, the Chihuahuan Desert is commonly referred to as a shrub desert, supporting barrel cactus, yucca, ocotillo, and the ubiquitous creosote bush.

Even though this area has been inhabited for thousands of years by native peoples, those first European explorers—the Spanish conquistadors, fettered by a mission from their king and their Church—must have questioned their loyalty and their faith as they forged into this harsh and unforgiving land. The explorers meandered along the path of the Rio Grande and ventured into what is now west Texas as early as 1581. By the end of the 16th century, the area, which is a few miles south of present-day El Paso, was colonized and dubbed El Paso del Norte. Unfortunately, few of the original buildings exist today since the earthen adobe structures built on the plains along the river simply washed away when it flooded.

Over time the land transferred from Spanish to Mexican control, and by 1848, it was American territory. El Paso flourished as a major stop for the famous Butterfield Overland Mail Stagecoach and later as a railroad town with each train bringing a steady stream of American emigrants. As the city developed—flush with cash from cattle and oil—transplanted easterners were determined to add a flair of sophistication to the simple adobe structures that had been predominant in the area for centuries. Today, El Paso and the surrounding communities boast nine different historic districts ranging in style from early-day Spanish Colonial and stately Georgian to Classical Revival mansions and elaborate turn-of-the-century Victorian homes.

While some citizens of El Paso were building fancy desert mansions, the residents of Mesilla, New Mexico just a few miles north along the Rio Grande, wanted nothing to do with their new country—the United States. Originally in Mexico, the village became part of this country with the 1853 Gadsden Purchase—a fact most villagers refused to recognize. They continued to live with the customs and culture of "old Mexico." Today, the low-slung rooflines of Old Mesilla's original adobe structures are visions of bygone days with soft earthen hues punctuated by weathered wooden gates and brightly painted grillwork. The town's historic plaza is lined with artisans' shops and galleries while the scent of authentic Southwest cuisine permeates the air.

You can experience the rugged Chihuahuan Desert by following Interstate 10 across west Texas and veering north at El Paso into New Mexico. At Las Cruces, you can take Interstate 25 heading north toward the vast grasslands around Albuquerque, or take Interstate 10 due west through the southwestern half of New Mexico, where the harsh terrain is dotted with natural wetlands. After crossing into Arizona, the Chihuahuan Desert gradually ends as the flora and fauna of the Sonoran Desert begins.

OPPOSITE TOP: **Colorful chiles contrast against an old adobe dwelling.** OPPOSITE BOTTOM: **Adobe buildings in Mesilla, New Mexico date around 1854 when the Gadsden Purchase made the small town a part of the United States.** ABOVE: **When New Mexico's official state flower, the yucca, blooms, its stalk of creamy white petals contrasts with its sharp, sword-like leaves.** RIGHT: **The sun, the heat, and an abundance of time take their toll on scenic artifacts from a lifestyle gone by.**

OPPOSITE: **Near Las Cruces, New Mexico, the Rio Grande meanders through the Chihuahuan Desert.** UPPER LEFT: **As El Paso, Texas flourished, simple adobe dwellings were shunned in favor of grand building styles popular in the east.** UPPER RIGHT: **Along with El Paso's large-scale traditional homes, water-thirsty grass lawns and non-native vegetation replaced desert terrain.** CENTER LEFT: **Mission-style homes with architectural details similar to old Spanish missions date from around 1890 to 1920. This classic example is in El Paso's Sunset Heights Historical District.** CENTER RIGHT: **By the 1920s, a Spanish revival swept the nation. El Paso architect Mabel Welch designed this classic Spanish Renaissance dwelling for Dr. and Mrs. Harry Leigh in 1929.** BOTTOM: **This elaborate El Paso mansion was featured in a local magazine in 1892.**

An Artist's Retreat

OPPOSITE: **After learning to plaster, Jo-an hand-formed the living room's built-in *bancos*, sculptural details, and corbels that blend into the ceiling's square *vigas*. Jo-an's colorful paintings and sculptures, inspired by the American Southwest and Latin America, often feature architectural elements of her home.** BOTTOM: **Twisted mesquite and locust trees frame the scenic patio vistas extending beyond the Rio Grande toward the rugged Organ Mountains.**

ERCHED ON A SECLUDED MESA north of Las Cruces, New Mexico, artist Jo-an Smith has created a dwelling that is as much her sculpture as it is her home. Soft, hand-formed adobe walls appear to grow from the rocky hillside, and the northern portion of the house is carved, cave-like, into the rugged terrain. To the south, sweeping views fan across the Rio Grande valley framed in the distance by the Organ Mountains' jagged profile.

For Jo-an, her home is a twenty-year work in progress—a canvas to be changed, redefined, and recreated. As an artist and craftsman, Jo-An supervised every detail, often frustrating workman with demands to reshape corners and edges to fit her vision. More often, she just did the work herself, forming sculptural details out of the adobe.

"I gravitate toward the same types of shapes—organic, rounded," explained Jo-an. "Many times my ideas overlap. I would use certain shapes in my paintings and then find myself recreating them as I worked on the house. Perhaps a jewelry design might inspire a detail on the chimney, and then later, the chimney detail may show up in one of my paintings."

For several years, Jo-an and her husband lived in South and Central America, an experience that continues to affect her artistic style. During their travels through Argentina, El Salvador, and Panama, the couple accumulated a wealth of native artifacts—colorful woven textiles are scattered throughout the house while delicate pottery and ancient wooden tools are dramatically displayed. Jo-an is particularly proud of the100-year-old French bronze of Don Quixote discovered in Buenos Aires, which is predominantly displayed in the living room.

But a glance around the house reveals artifacts aren't just on display, they are an integral part of the home's design as Jo-an diligently incorporated features to showcase her collection of antique doors, columns, and other architectural artifacts gathered on her many excursions. "Openings were created to accommodate several old mesquite doors and shutters, and in the living room are two of my favorite discoveries—two hand carved Honduras mahogany doors," said Jo-an. At every turn throughout the house, Jo-an's unique blend of art and architecture is evident.

With an artist's eye, she also approached the ceilings in each room as an opportunity to experiment. In the living room, pine planks are angled between each beam. The *latillas* in the bedroom were fashioned from grape stakes, while rows of desert willow lay between the *vigas* down the hallway. Even the bathroom ceiling softly rounds down into the surrounding adobe walls.

The living room is an ever-changing gallery of Jo-an's latest paintings, while niches and columns display her sensual sculptures. But it is the richness of the home's design that beckons attention. So while it is true Jo-an lives amidst her art—it's also apparent that she lives within her art.

OPPOSITE: **Artifacts from Mexico line the hallway leading to guest quarters and a passive solar sunroom. Accenting the ceiling are** *latillas* **fashioned from peeled and dried desert willows found near the Rio Grande.** ABOVE: **The adobe compound appears to grow out of its perch on a rocky bluff. This softly curving wall becomes part of the fireplace.** RIGHT: **Antique mesquite doors, complete with original hardware, lead into the master bedroom and study.**

An Ancestral Adobe

ANN ENRIQUEZ has an unusual connection to her ancestors given America's young history. The home she occupies with husband Gaspar was built by her relatives in the 1680s and has passed from generation to generation for over 300 years.

Along with other Spanish pioneers immigrating to the New World in the early 17th century, Ann's family trekked northward along the Rio Grande, settling in what is now Santa Fe, New Mexico. But by 1680, local turmoil caused the residents to abandon Santa Fe for the more established Spanish communities near present-day San Elizario, Texas. Today, their architectural legacy can be seen in the simple dwellings that still remain, and the Enriquez home offers a perfect tour through the historic Spanish style prevalent throughout the region.

For nearly two and a half centuries, little was done to change the Enriquez home—the original dirt floors were maintained, the plumbing was left outdoors, and the cooking was done over a large open hearth. In the 1950s, Ann's grandmother sparingly added a few modern conveniences such as a small indoor bathroom, electricity, tile floors, and a few necessary kitchen appliances. More recently, Ann and Gaspar have installed heating and air conditioning as well as a protective covering over the old roof to insure against water exposure, since water virtually melts the adobe.

Unfortunately, not much of the original European furniture survives. "Over the years, family members just took items with them as they moved in and out," said Ann. But she doesn't mind, as all the details of the past remain imbedded within their home—the original *vigas*, the antique doors, the protective courtyard. The couple is content to live in their 320-year-old adobe home amidst the history and spirits of Ann's Spanish ancestors.

OPPOSITE TOP: A protective wall shelters the old adobe compound, which is surrounded by native cactus and shaded by large, old trees. OPPOSITE BOTTOM: In the 1680s, Ann's ancestors relied on locally available materials to construct their home. Tall cottonwood trees and desert willows growing along the nearby Rio Grande provided the ceiling's *vigas* and *latillas*. RIGHT: Until a few years ago, this covered porch along the front of the dwelling still had its original packed dirt floor.

Luxury Meets Longhorns

MANEUVERING ACROSS THE RUGGED Chihuahuan Desert terrain miles from the nearest hint of civilization, the notion that anyone would deliberately settle here is impossible to fathom. But over a century ago, this remote region was a bustling colony ruled by one of the West's earliest cattle barons. Now decades later, the authentically restored adobe dwellings and genuine Texas hospitality lure guests to bask in the luxurious solitude of Cibolo Creek Ranch, found near the rippling Rio Grande along the Mexican border, just northwest of scenic Big Bend National Park.

On a mission to locate a "ranch with character" for a private retreat, Houston businessman John Poindexter happened upon this sprawling 30,000-acre dilapidated compound nestled amidst the Chinati Mountains and was immediately captivated by the spirit of the land. "The place was abused and neglected," explained John. "Fences had crumbled, trails were washed out, and years of erosion and over-grazing had taken their toll." Also, sections of the ranch's three original 19th century adobe forts were in ruins. But unable to shake his fascination with the pioneer romance of the ranch, John spent the next two years on a quest to acquire the land.

The ranch's history, much of which is popular area folklore, began in the mid-1800s when local

freighter Milton Faver recognized the business potential of nearby Fort Davis and purchased the land along Cibolo Creek. Faver eventually constructed three unique adobe forts as business headquarters for his extensive cattle, sheep, goat, and agricultural operations. By 1880, the ranch boasted 20,000 longhorn cattle and countless acres of spring-fed orchards.

As a pioneer of early day cattle drives, Milton Faver is presumed to be the inspiration for character Gil Faver featured in the popular 1960s television series *Rawhide*. Although Faver died in 1889, his wife and son retained the property until their deaths in the early 1900s. During the 20th century, Cibolo Creek Ranch passed through a series of hands, gradually falling into disrepair until John Poindexter came to the rescue in 1990.

What occurred over the next four years is a testimony to John's perseverance, commitment, and his own admittedly "particular irrationality" to a historically accurate restoration. With input from the Texas State Historical Commission, John was adamant about maintaining the original integrity of the old dwellings while adding the modern conveniences of today's lifestyle.

As the building research began, John focused on the surrounding environment, reintroducing longhorn cattle, horses, buffalo, and even an occasional camel in deference to the U.S. Army's failed experiment from the 1850s of using camels instead of horses in the desert Southwest. Miles of fence were reconstructed using the same rocks that had tumbled from their original perch, while the ranch's old *acequias* (irrigation canals) once again delivered water from the natural springs.

In the meantime, antique photographs, historical

LEFT: To create the ambiance of a 19th century interior within El Cibilo's spacious dining area, antique oil lamps were electrically retrofitted providing a subtle warm glow. OPPOSITE: An array of Spanish, Mexican, and ranch-style antiques blend with custom doors, adobe tile, and colorful weavings.

archives, and interviews with the area's old-timers helped identify the configuration of eroded walls and area gardens. John went to almost fanatical lengths to assure the project's accuracy, even searching through the Library of Congress. "That's where we found photos allowing us to determine the height of the original doorsteps," said John, who's visited virtually every adobe structure from Colorado to Texas. Using a 1930's photograph, even Faver's hilltop mausoleum was reconstructed.

New structures were crafted from hand-formed adobe using window and door details replicated from old photos, including custom-forged nails. Clever details conceal electrical wiring and air conditioning units. Even modern-day bathrooms

are hidden behind faux-armoire doors. To complete the splendor of a 19th century hacienda, John scoured the country in search of period Mexican, Spanish, and old ranch furnishings. In the end, John's attention to detail paid off with the ranch garnering three listings on the National Register of Historic Places and five Texas Historical Markers.

Each of the three resurrected forts offers a distinctly different environment. The largest of Faver's strongholds, El Cibolo, houses a library, small chapel, and museum filled with the area's ranch, military, and Native American artifacts. It is flanked by the hacienda-style guest rooms and a heated swimming pool.

Just a few miles down a scenic gravel road is La Cienega, reportedly Mick Jagger's favorite ranch getaway, featuring a small museum and four spacious guest rooms within the generous confines of the 140-year-old fort. All the rooms include fireplaces but no television or phone to disturb the peaceful ambiance.

Surrounded by remote wilderness crawling with illusive black bears, La Morita is the third and smallest fortress, providing the ultimate in desert solitude with no electricity or communication besides the ranch's two-way radio.

Big names such as Larry Hagman and Lone Star native Dan Rather frequent the ranch, and a number of celebrities have chosen to tie-the-knot at this remote desert hideaway, including Dixie Chick Emily Erwin. But in most cases, star-gazing typically involves sitting around a big Texas bonfire, listening to the soft strains of a guitar serenade, and gazing listlessly into the expansive twinkling night skies. The old cattle baron would surely be pleased.

TOP: A spring fed brook ripples through the courtyard at El Cibolo creating the soothing sounds of running water audible within each of the hacienda-style rooms. From the covered veranda, the fort's main tower is visible. BOTTOM: Stark shadows stripe the interior courtyard at La Morita, left partially restored at the request of the Texas Historical Commission. With only oil lamps and a wood stove for light and heat, romantically inclined guests often request this remote hideaway. OPPOSITE: Desert vistas including the Chinati Mountains are visible from El Cibolo's heated pool. Although guests typically eat meals together in the historical dining room, custom cuisine is often served at the poolside veranda.

Defining Details

BUILDINGS IN THE SOUTHWEST have long been identified by their architectural character and design arising out of a blend of Native American practicality, Old World Spanish craftsmanship, and Anglo-American ingenuity. Although modern technology negates the necessity of once vital building techniques, it is these details that continue to define Southwest desert style.

Interior courtyards, originally built for protection, have become soulful private retreats. Inviting corner fireplaces, once essential for cooking and warmth, remain popular design additions. And arched openings with heavy protective doors and forged iron gates and window grills, while no longer required for safety, provide a unique southwestern flavor.

The subtle hues of local earthen materials are contrasted with bright colors of Mexican descent— turquoise and bright blues accented by the deep red of a chile ristra. *Vigas, latillas,* and other ornate features, once an intricate part of the building structure, remain favorite methods for ceiling design and are now used purely for decoration.

Wildly colorful Mexican-made tiles are extensively used, especially in kitchens and bathrooms, and even as tabletops. Creatively crafted forged iron is preferred for staircase railings, while hand-hewn doors add character to new construction.

Styles have now become so intertwined that it is often difficult to define a specific period. A rustic Mexican-made bench or pottery collection is quite at home in a contemporary desert dwelling. And large expanses of energy efficient windows now often replace the small, deep-set openings of the territorial adobe of a century ago.

Even if you live in one of today's prevalent red-tiled roof tract homes, it is possible to create your own desert style through a series of well-crafted details. Walls can be faux-finished to give the illusion of undulating adobe. Hammered ironwork and hand-forged metal add an Old World look when incorporated as drapery hardware. Mexican-made tile, etched glass, handcrafted furniture, Native American or Old West artifacts, built-in niches, and rusted metal finishes are just a few examples of the subtle details employed in today's desert dwellings.

OPPOSITE BOTTOM: **El Paso historian Barbara Rees still resides in the Spanish Renaissance home built for her parents in 1929. Old beams salvaged from a dismantled bridge in Juarez, Mexico were elaborately carved and are showcased throughout the home.** OPPOSITE TOP: **Richly faux finished walls, a leaded glass window, and dramatic native boulders blend elements of desert design.** ABOVE: **Details on the hand-wrought iron handrail reflect the carved wood element imbedded in the plaster.** RIGHT: **This classic Southwest staircase incorporates wrought iron details accented by Mexican tile on the front of each stair.**

The Sonoran Desert

THE SONORAN DESERT covers 120,000 miles of arid land encompassing southern Arizona, southeastern California, and extending south into Mexico. The most formidable symbol of the Sonoran Desert is the stately saguaro cactus, which is found nowhere else in the world. Jagged mountain ranges cut through the sun-baked landscape, while "sky islands" thrust upward thousands of vertical feet from the desert floor providing a unique environment for flora and fauna. Just 35 miles northeast of sunny Tucson, Arizona is the nation's southernmost ski area. The pine forests and fifteen ski slopes of Mount Lemmon Ski Valley offer a winter experience minutes from the sea of sparkling swimming pools in Tucson.

110 miles west of Tucson is Ventana Cave, the earliest known residence of man in this region. The original inhabitants enjoyed rainfall of at least 40 inches, which is almost four times the present rate. Giant sloths and wooly mammoths were plentiful for hunting and the moderate climate made life comfortable. It took thousands of years—10,000, in fact—before evidence shows the first attempts at architecture.

Around A.D. 300, small villages of single-family dwellings first appeared in northern Arizona and New Mexico. By A.D. 700, the small pit houses and huts had transformed into well-designed pueblos, housing multiple families. Hundreds of pueblos dotted the Southwest, carved into the sides of cliffs or situated beside streams. Many were small, but some loomed over five stories with more than a thousand residents. The cultures were remarkably similar with many pueblos existing peaceably near each other.

Ruins from the ancient Hohokam culture in central Arizona indicate multiple-storied, elaborate pueblos with sophisticated ballcourts over 200 feet long. They crafted unique red on buff pottery and weaved cotton and lace. But it was their civil engineering feats that continue to define these

pre-historic people. By this time, this region had evolved into an arid, hot desert so the Hohokam built miles of canals—some 30 feet wide and seven feet deep. Water from the nearby Gila River irrigated acres of desert terrain, transforming it into lush farmland. To date, over 250 miles of canals have been traced.

The next evidence of spectacular desert architecture can be attributed to the Spaniards. While most Spanish explorers followed the path of the Rio Grande up to northern New Mexico where Santa Fe was founded in 1609, others ventured along a route through the Sonoran Desert.

The Spanish colonization of the northern Sonoran Desert was minimal compared to that in New Mexico, although a string of twenty-nine missions were successfully built thanks to the influence of a Jesuit missionary, Father Kino. Today, most of the original missions are in ruins, but two remain in good repair—Tumacacori Mission and the "White Dove of the Desert" San Xavier Del Bac, both of which are just south of Tucson.

Four hundred years after the Hohokam abandoned their canals, American entrepreneurs began using them again, founding a series of businesses along their banks and ultimately establishing the city of Phoenix. As the new town developed, wealthy residents shunned native adobe architecture and turned instead to the nation's popular Victorian style. The Rosson House, a prominent Victorian home built in 1895, is the cornerstone of Historic Heritage Square in downtown Phoenix where ten historic homes and buildings from the turn of the century fill an old city block. Desert summers

LEFT: This 1908 photograph of Casa Grande Ruins National Monument south of Phoenix, Arizona highlights the 700-year-old four-story solid earth structure. Believed to be a watchtower or observatory built by the prehistoric Hohokam using layers of caliche mud, walls at the base are 4.5-feet thick. OPPOSITE: South of Tucson, Arizona the Mission San Xavier Del Bac, built in the late 1700s, is considered one of the finest examples of mission architecture in the United States.

prompted unique architectural adaptations; one house features a summer sleeping porch while another was built with an additional sixteen inches between the ceiling and the attic to aid in summer ventilation. The Rosson House is now a museum filled with original Victorian furnishings, while restaurants, tearooms, art galleries, the Arizona Doll and Toy Museum, and historical displays fill the other homes.

Along Interstate 10 east of Tucson the Chihuahuan Desert begins its transition into Sonoran Desert terrain and the saguaro cactus gradually begins to appear. I-10 continues northwest through Tucson and Phoenix where it turns west again and stretches across miles of pristine desert toward the western edge near Palm Springs, California. Interstate 8 intersects I-10 just south of Phoenix and heads west through the sand dunes of Yuma, Arizona—where Star Wars was filmed—and into the southern desert regions of California. In Tucson, I-19 drops south to the border town of Nogales where miles of Sonoran Desert extend into Mexico.

OPPOSITE: Downtown Phoenix, Arizona bathed in moonlight. ABOVE: Growing about a foot per decade, the saguaro doesn't develop its first arm until it is fifty to seventy-five years old. Towering up to fifty feet and weighing in at 1500 pounds, the stately cactus can live for 200 years. RIGHT: Built in 1895, the Victorian-style Rosson House originally cost $7,525 and was one of the prominent homes in early day Phoenix, Arizona. Today, the restored home is filled with period antiques and is one of eleven historical structures comprising Heritage Square in downtown Phoenix.

A Jewel in the Desert

OPPOSITE: **Phil's cozy office reflects an eclectic mix of furnishings and accessories including the desktop that was fashioned from an antique door. Walls are hand-plastered, then glazed with a deep red base followed by a hand-rubbed umber oil glaze.** BELOW: **Blooming desert flowers intertwine with native agaves and yucca against a backdrop of soft adobe walls, antique gates, and the Tortilita Mountains.**

I N THE FOOTHILLS of the Tortolita Mountains, about forty-five minutes northeast of Tucson, Arizona, a little adobe dwelling perched on a ridge with sweeping views of the surrounding desert sat waiting to be discovered. So when interior designer Linda Robinson decided one day to explore the rugged terrain, it must have been fate that led her down a remote dirt road, twisting and winding until it dead-ended in front of the secluded residence.

There it sat, not exactly the vision of elegance. An outhouse indicated the lack of plumbing, a couple car batteries and solar panels provided electricity, and nearby, a tank and a well appeared the only water source. But Linda was immediately intrigued with the rustic abode and its locale. Then she noticed a realtor's sign.

As a partner in the Tucson design firm, Robinson & Shades Design Group, Linda's days are ensconced in providing clients with detailed elaborate design solutions. And her husband, Phil Perry, owner of Perry/Fuld Design & Manufacturing, designs and produces a line of metal furnishings and ironwork carried in some of the nation's top designer showrooms and is featured in prestigious catalogs such as Pottery Barn.

"But our personal lifestyle is very casual and comfortable. I just didn't want to live in a big decorated house. In fact, we'd been searching for some acreage out of the city, and after returning to that little adobe house with a realtor, I knew I wanted it. But I was still overwhelmed with doubts," said Linda. Ultimately, she credits Phil's encouragement and his confidence in her design ability as the deciding factor to purchase the property.

Throughout the planning process Linda's philosophy remained unfaltering—to create a rambling old ranch house using organic, native materials while blending indoor and outdoor living spaces.

Even with years of architectural and construction knowledge and the experience of a "hands-on"

designer, this remodel was more challenging than anticipated. Since the existing house was really just a square room with a kitchen, the first phase consisted of adding on a living room, bedroom, and laundry along with the required plumbing, electrical wiring, and kitchen necessities.

Soon, it was apparent that meeting contractors twice a day so far from town wasn't practical. Linda also realized she wanted to be onsite overseeing the craftsmanship, so the couple moved in with just a bed and a couple chairs set up in the kitchen.

As the project progressed, Linda was relentless in her attention to detail. Hand-plastered walls, kept rough and irregular, were stained and then wiped with an umber glaze for a rich weathered finish. Desert rocks, painstakingly gathered and hauled to the building site, blended into flooring and fireplace details. Openings, designed around antique doors, also camouflaged entertainment areas, while Phil's company produced an array of custom hardware designed to enhance the old ranch house ambiance.

"As I contemplated the overall design, I wanted to maintain the character of the original dwelling while keeping it as a central part of the house," explained Linda. The room's eight-foot ceiling creates a cozy farmhouse effect especially as it transitions into the expansive eleven-foot heights of the newly constructed adjoining rooms. When Linda discovered that the existing kitchen cabinets were made at a nearby sawmill, she commissioned the company to duplicate the old design and she expanded the cabinetry. The kitchen also provides the only access to the master bedroom and Linda's office, adding to the appearance that the house has been added onto over the years.

Large expanses of glass highlight the home's spectacular desert views and the rooms easily flow into several outdoor living areas. "We especially enjoy the outdoor spaces, whether we are alone watching a sunset or entertaining a large group," said Linda, who approached the design of the two courtyards and terraced patio with the same fervor and diligence as each of the interior spaces.

Adobe walls and antique gates shelter the courtyards and gardens from desert critters that might wander in uninvited; mountain lions and rattlesnakes are native to this area. *Portales,* or covered patios, provide a shady respite from the desert sun while the gardens are accented with native cactus contrasted by the brilliant pinks, deep yellows, and bright purples of blooming desert flowers.

For Linda and Phil, their secluded home is a retreat, a sanctuary of serenity carefully crafted from the humble beginnings of an old adobe dwelling—their jewel in the desert.

ABOVE: **Appearing weathered and rusted, these iron handles were custom designed and manufactured by Phil's company.** OPPOSITE: **The kitchen is part of the original adobe structure, along with its eight-foot ceilings, pine cabinets, and vintage gas range. By using shotgun blasts to distress the exposed cabinet doors and blending smooth concrete counters next to deliberately broken-edged tiles, the island appears from the same era even though it was added during the renovation.**

LEFT: The patterned dining room floor fashioned with old bricks and rocks gathered from the surrounding desert is original to the old adobe structure as is the beamed eight-foot wooden ceiling. Linda's pewter collection is displayed above the expansive window overlooking the courtyard. ABOVE: Corrugated tin accentuates the dining room fireplace. OPPOSITE: Large windows on three sides of the master bedroom offer spectacular desert views. A built-in plaster cabinet was designed around antique doors. The iron and copper bed is from Phil's company.

OPPOSITE: With eleven-foot ceilings, the living room's hand-plastered walls were purposely kept uneven with an umber oil glaze accenting the irregularities. Antique doors hide the entertainment center. The metal table, fireplace screen, and wall sconce adjacent to the stone fireplace are products from Perry/Fuld Design & Manufacturing. ABOVE: Antique doors are utilized throughout the house often camouflaging entertainment areas and other modern day functional spaces. RIGHT: Bathed in candlelight, this small letter writing alcove off the living room blends antiques and reproductions in elegant hacienda style. The tin roof sparkles from the courtyard beyond.

LEFT: In the guest bathroom, Linda simulated elements of an antique wash basin by utilizing an old buffet. A granite bowl, crafted with a rough chiseled exterior and smooth polished interior, was installed appearing as though it sits on the cabinet. ABOVE: Over the years, antique doors of all sizes were collected and incorporated throughout the house. OPPOSITE: This patio, one of several outdoor living areas, is a perfect spot for entertaining. Often, after a summer monsoon, waterfalls pour over the rocky cliffs into the sandy wash below.

Sustainable Architecture

MODERN EARTH ARCHITECTURE has seen a recent resurgence in popularity. Historic building techniques such as adobe, rammed earth, and straw bale have stood the test of time in this harsh climate and are now being used as the cornerstone in many elaborate and expensive desert homes.

Using earth and water to create adobe bricks was a technique new to the indigenous cultures of America's desert regions. For centuries, dwellings were fashioned from stone and mud, but it was the Spanish, upon their arrival in the 1500s, who introduced the method of casting wet mud into bricks. The mud mixture was poured into forms and left in the desert sun to dry, usually for about 30 days. Although a current standard brick is typically ten by fourteen inches and four inches thick, adobe walls built by the Spanish were more than twice that.

Rammed earth construction appears to be as ancient as adobe with excavations in China revealing remnants of rammed earth buildings dating to the seventh century. Instead of using individual bricks, rammed earth walls are created by erecting two parallel wood frames that act as a mold, which are then completely filled with a compacted or rammed mud mixture.

During the 1800s, pioneers forging their way across the Midwestern plains, used bales of straw to construct homes, farm buildings, and even schools. Recently, straw bale construction has gained popularity in the Southwest due to its low cost, energy efficiency, and easy building technique. Window and door openings are simply carved out of the stacked straw bales with a chainsaw. Finally, layers of stucco are hand-applied, creating undulating thick walls and soft curves reminiscent of the adobe style prevalent in this region.

Earth materials are also environmentally friendly, storing the sun's heat by day while radiating warmth inward during cool desert nights. Earth walls don't emit toxins, are fire and insect resistant, and can be constructed using locally available materials. As a bonus, modern techniques of plastering and sealing have eliminated most of the constant upkeep previously required. In all, today's earth dwellings are perfectly suited for desert life.

OPPOSITE: Architect Frank Lloyd Wright used rocks from the desert floor and sand from desert washes during the construction of Taliesin West, his wintertime home and studio in Scottsdale, Arizona. ABOVE: Utilizing colorful accent colors, this charming chapel in Elgin, Arizona was engineered with straw bale construction. TOP RIGHT: Bodie and Nancy Robins' rammed earth home was designed to meet the restrictive architectural covenants in this historic Tucson, Arizona neighborhood. BOTTOM RIGHT: Although this home appears to be a traditional adobe dwelling, it actually was constructed using straw bale techniques.

Old World Renaissance

OPPOSITE: **Since the ground floor has no support walls, wooden beams were hollowed out and slipped over the structural steel beams, then hand-carved, stained, and painted. Notice how the beam design subltly reflects the color and pattern of the sunburst pillow below.** BOTTOM: **Elements of an old adobe mission were created by blending a protective iron gate and antique bell discovered in Mexico.**

WHEN INTERIOR DESIGNER TONY SUTTON was first approached by his clients, their mandate was clear—to create a vacation home blending into the desert surroundings that would convey a striking sense of Southwest history and the traditions of its people. Tony, known for his innovative custom work, has spent nearly twenty years as the owner and lead designer of Est Est, Inc., a multi-faceted interior design firm in Scottsdale, Arizona. Designated as a "Master of the Southwest" by *Phoenix Home & Garden* Magazine, Tony expanded on his own experience by assembling a project team of related professionals who merged their skills and successfully accomplished his client's design challenge.

As the design development phase progressed, the ground floor, which consisted of the entryway, living room, dining area, family room, kitchen, and breakfast area, became essentially one "great room" that flowed from one area to the other, with only a half-wall providing any type of partition. Without any support walls, steel ceiling beams were necessary, which then presented a design dilemma—how to disguise the utilitarian beams.

"So we brought even larger wood beams onto the job site and had them canoed out. Then, I worked closely with the craftsman as we defined each detail and custom finish. Once installed, the steel beams were completely camouflaged," explained Tony.

And they didn't stop there; this attention to craftsmanship and detail can be found in every room. Sparkling windowpanes with inset glass beads border the living room's sunburst fireplace. The half-wall dividing the kitchen and dining area showcase Mexican plates recessed into the plaster, creating a unique "south-of-the-border" feel. In the family room, architectural niches surround the built-in entertainment area that remains hidden when not in use by hand-carved custom doors with a distressed finish. And throughout the home, a special pigmented plaster covers the drywall.

On the exterior, as the initial plaster began to crack and peel, as it always does, colored plaster was applied creating the irregular finish of aged patina. The exterior also boasts custom iron gates with specially designed handles and an antique bell that was discovered in Old Mexico. The custom door hardware was so impressive that a local hardware company has incorporated it into their line.

In the custom of old Spanish dwellings, the house wraps around an inner courtyard with an entry into each wing. A Jacuzzi sits at the base of a spiral staircase leading to a second floor master suite, which offers magnificent views of north Scottsdale's Pinnacle Peak on one side and a panoramic vista of the valley and city lights on the other. Two guest casitas flank the courtyard. An exterior fireplace blazes near the courtyard's compact rectangular swimming pool, customized with "resistance jets" that can be adjusted to manage the amount of exercise desired. As a finishing touch, native plants gracefully merge with the adjacent desert wash.

With architectural details in place, they turned to the fine interior details. Light fixtures and custom furnishings were designed and artwork was commissioned to blend with the home's finishes and colors.

As for Tony's clients, when the nearly three-year process drew to a close, they were thrilled with the results. "Selecting talented professionals and then following their advice was our biggest accomplishment," the couple exclaimed. "They gave us a home reminiscent of the Old World, and filled it with the conveniences of modern-day life."

OPPOSITE: The entry hall's flagstone flooring is accented with natural riverbed stones imbedded in the grout. An antique hand-carved chest sits under a painting appropriately titled, "I said, Whoa Horse!" ABOVE: Hand-carved pocket doors add ambiance to the family room while neatly camouflaging the entertainment area. Built-in niches feature museum quality Native American artifacts. The fireplace is elevated so it can be enjoyed from the kitchen. RIGHT: An Ed Mell original hangs over the console, which is accented by details incorporating the ranch brand of the owners.

OPPOSITE: A half-wall featuring Mexican plates recessed into the plaster separates the kitchen and dining areas. The heavily distressed gallery table is custom designed with accent color insets.

ABOVE AND RIGHT: A natural granite boulder from the area appears to grow from the flagstone floor to support the hand-chiseled flagstone counter-top. The pewter sink and brushed metal apron blend with the unique lead and copper frame of the custom mirror.

A Dream By Design

PART OF THE SOUTHWEST'S ALLURE is its unique interior design and architecture. But desert newcomers are often overwhelmed with unfamiliar styles and material choices. So whether you're remodeling or relocating, seeking professional design advice is an investment that can save time, frustration, and money.

The first step is to define the scope of your project and that largely depends on identifying your budget. If you are moving, time constraints also need to be addressed. Then spend some time looking at design styles and finishes, keeping examples of your likes and dislikes. Once you've determined if you'll be building, remodeling, or redecorating, then begin your search for professional assistance.

Depending on your project's scope, you might hire one or several professionals. Interior designer vs. decorator, landscaper vs. landscape architect—just trying to decipher this terminology can be frustrating. But since there is often an overlap of roles, it pays to do your homework and understand the different services available. On larger projects a creative team may be assembled so each design decision is coordinated along with the construction.

Because of their professional training, architects, interior designers, and landscape architects provide creative services that go beyond just the aesthetics of a space. Function, efficiency, and safety concerns are combined with the basic design to create entire interior and exterior environments.

Decorators typically confine their services to "surface decoration"—the selection of flooring, paint, furnishings, window coverings, etc., whereas interior designers offer a broad scope of services from developing the initial floor plan, to detailing custom cabinetry, fireplaces, and other architectural elements. Interior designers also specify lighting, plumbing fixtures, and finish materials. Their projects range from design development to the specification and installation of furnishings, art, and accessories.

This same comparison can be applied to landscapers vs. landscape architects. Landscapers usually supply and install plants, trees, and lawns. Some also provide irrigation systems, special rock or brick features, garden edging, etc. Experienced landscapers also might offer ideas or opinions on plant selections and locations, but it is the landscape architect who creates entire exterior environments. Landscape architects often plan and incorporate outdoor living areas, swimming pools, plant specification, exterior lighting, pathways, fence materials, and other exterior elements.

ABOVE: **Professional designers often produce a presentation board, indicating the various colors, finishes, and materials being specified for a client. Scottsdale, Arizona interior design firm Est Est, Inc. created this presentation board and the end results using these finishes is shown.**
OPPOSITE TOP: **Architects, interior designers, and other professionals generally rely on an up-to-date extensive resource library.** OPPOSITE BOTTOM: **This conference room at interior design firm Est Est, Inc. provides ample space for clients and the design team to review construction plans and evaluate finish and furnishing options.**

Architects and landscape architects are licensed in all fifty states while interior designers are currently licensed in eighteen states. Three professional organizations offer extensive information about their specific design field: American Society of Interior Designers (ASID), American Institute of Architects (AIA), and American Society of Landscape Architects (ASLA). Education, professional experience, and rigorous testing are required to use these appellations and members are governed by a strict code of ethics (See Resources, page 160).

Once you have decided what kind of professional service you need, a good way to start is by getting referrals from friends or relatives. If that is not an option, take some time and call a few firms—ask for references, years of experience with your type of project, and determine whether they have additional technical expertise, special credentials, or are a member of a trade association.

As with most professionals, fee structures for design services vary. Options include a fixed fee, an hourly rate, compensation based on the square footage of the project, or a percentage calculated on the total construction/project costs, and a combination of compensation methods is not unusual.

Lastly, don't base your final decision on price alone. The creative process is time consuming and requires an enormous amount of personal interaction. Make sure you're comfortable with the business methods and style of the person or firm you hire, and then ask yourself if you'll enjoy spending a lot of time together.

A Home with a View

OPPOSITE: Vast windows offer expansive desert views from the living room. Coved plaster ceilings and accent beams blend into the massive fireplace, fashioned from indigenous Arizona rock.

BOTTOM: A flagstone path winds toward the custom wood and glass front door accented by a stone surround. Imitating a desert stream, water meanders amidst the boulders lining the entry courtyard's walkway.

LIKE MANY CHICAGO RESIDENTS, this semi-retired couple decided to leave the cold, northern winters behind. But not wanting to make a permanent break from their family and friends, they chose to build a winter retreat amidst the sunny skies and convenient amenities of Scottsdale, Arizona.

After searching the desert region, they settled in north Scottsdale in an exclusive golf resort development. Bordered by lush green fairways in the shadow of the McDowell Mountains, their desert abode gradually took shape.

As they contemplated the home's concept, interior designers Tony Sutton and Marilynn Nicola were commissioned to develop the plans. "While we were looking for creative solutions and unique furnishings, we also wanted the home to display a regional flavor," the owners said. Since the couple didn't intend to use any furnishings or art from their Chicago home, the designers were free to approach the project unencumbered by the restrictions of existing styles, sizes, or colors.

"Throughout the planning process, our goal was to radiate the strength of character and purpose inherent in those who settled the Southwest. In keeping with that philosophy, the overall effect had to be strong, yet subtle and understated," explained Tony.

Because the lot offered unparalleled views in all directions, Tony and architect Lash McDaniels began the development phase by challenging themselves to incorporate each panoramic vista within the architecture of the home.

Pinnacle Peak, the area's defining rugged landmark, is perfectly framed in a custom arched window, accented with decorative iron and seeded glass. The unusual window design is also featured in the nearby dining room, which opens onto the front garden. Large expanses of glass lining the living room offer visions of blazing western sunsets followed by a mass of twinkling city lights across

the desert horizon. Virtually every room in the spacious four-bedroom 5,500 square foot house provides grand desert views.

In the Southwest style of an old hacienda, a lush desert oasis courtyard protects the front entry. A canopy of palo verde trees softens the desert sun as water ripples around large native boulders lining the flagstone pathway, simulating the lazy current of a desert stream.

The flagstone continues from the pathway and flows through the entry, stairs, hallways, and kitchen. Artisan stonemasons gathered indigenous Arizona stone to create the living room's stunning rock fireplace. Hand-carved wood details, inset into the plaster walls, create another southwestern architectural element, and aspects of its geometric design are repeated in the custom wrought iron handrails.

Rounded corners and irregular angles mimic the hand-formed walls of an old adobe. Simple arched ceilings are accented with hand-hewn *vigas* and recessed lighting, while furniture is tucked into custom designed niches. Light color tones maintained throughout the home accentuate the natural hues of the wood, stone, and rock, blending perfectly with the custom furnishings and art.

And when the desert sun recedes, the couple often relaxes near their outdoor fireplace, gazing past the saguaro cactus that are framed in vivid pinks and purples of an Arizona sunset.

Understanding the time required to create a work of art, the owners committed almost three years to the design and construction of their

Sonoran Desert retreat. And so, each year, as they leave the winter's swirling winds and blowing snow behind and settle into their sunny desert lifestyle, it is with an appreciation of those early pioneers who forged into the Southwest, creating a legacy of desert style.

ABOVE: Custom designed shelves feature collectibles and accessories emphasized by low voltage lighting. Custom hardware is featured on the doors leading into the area. OPPOSITE: A hand-carved horse from Mexico stands guard over the entry hall accented by a colorful Kilim rug and alder table tucked into a niche designed around the table's dimensions.

OPPOSITE: Elements of southwestern style blend to create a casual breakfast room from the built-in plaster *banco* to the gently arched ceiling to the custom-carved columns. Western artist Howard Post was commissioned to provide the painting over the sofa. ABOVE: Beams were positioned beneath the arched hallway ceiling causing the skylights to cast dramatic desert shadows. RIGHT: A hand-painted buffet sits beneath the decorative iron window framing the area's signature landmark, Pinnacle Peak.

OPPOSITE: The native stone fireplace is the living room's focal point accented by a custom iron fireplace screen. Rustic doors fold back into the stone mass revealing a state of the art entertainment system. ABOVE: Architectural hand-carved wood detailing is embedded in the plaster on each side of this entry foyer niche, creating a vertical element. In the ceiling beyond, recessed lighting is hidden above the *vigas* accenting the arched plaster spines. RIGHT: This arched deep-set window integrates modern elements of an old adobe. Using a southwestern design, the etched glass perfectly frames the desert terrain.

Palm Springs Modern Style

As the Sonoran Desert edges west over the Colorado River into California, rainfall decreases by almost two-thirds, equaling around three inches per year. Even the desert-hardy Saguaro cactus won't survive here naturally. Often referred to as the Colorado Desert, this harsh, arid region became popular in the 1920s and 30s when Hollywood producers found it to be the perfect filming location for productions set in Africa and the Mediterranean.

Early Hollywood moguls spurred Palm Springs' initial development with Darryl Zanuck, Jack Warner, and Al Jolson building Spanish-style haciendas or sprawling ranch homes as their weekend and winter retreats. By the end of the 1930s, a handful of modernist and Art Deco homes also dotted the Palm Springs landscape.

The desert oasis continued to flourish in the 1940s and 50s as a favored getaway spot for the Hollywood crowd. Frank Sinatra, whose home included a piano shaped swimming pool, Bob Hope, Lucy and Desi, Bing Crosby, Liberace, Clark Gable, Kirk Douglas, and Walt Disney were among Palm Springs' glamorous part-time residents. The growing popularity of golf inspired the development of lush desert courses with elaborate country clubs, and many celebrities opted for homes built along the golf course fairways—an innovative concept at the time.

These new homes were among the first to welcome Europe's new International Style, where steel, rock, and cement were the favored building materials. Large expanses of glass offered pristine desert views, and the homes, now perfectly suited for their environment, were sleek, open, and bright.

National design magazines from Architectural Digest to House and Garden regularly featured the modern homes of the Palm Springs' rich and famous, introducing new building materials and modernist styles to the rest of the nation. Over the course of three decades, from the 1940s to the 1960s, Palm Springs spawned one of the most significant concentrations of modernist architecture in the world, much of which was designed by architects Albert Frey, E. Stewart Williams, Donald Wexler, and William F. Cody.

But by the late 1970s, the modernist homes and buildings looked tired and outdated. As the city languished, several of these properties were demolished, making way for shopping malls and parking lots. Then, the 1990s brought a renewed historical interest in mid-century modern architecture.

Don Wexler's prototype steel homes designed in 1961 are now highly coveted, and modernist fans prize George Alexander's 1950s tract homes, often renovating them back to their original condition. The era's revival is so popular that numerous retail stores even specialize in modern period furnishings.

ABOVE: **Architect Albert Frey's 1963 small glass house is virtually transparent. Here the bed is visible in the corner.** OPPOSITE TOP: **Frey's unique glass and metal home is perched on the edge of a boulder-strewn hillside overlooking Palm Springs. The glass wall slides open masking the divisions between indoor and outdoor areas.** OPPOSITE BOTTOM: **Typical of the modernist tract homes built by the Alexander Company, the personal home of the late Bob Alexander is a popular stop on the city's mid-century tours, recognized not only for its modernist "butterfly" roofline but also as the honeymoon getaway for Elvis and Priscilla Presley.**

Off the Beaten Path

Nestled within the rolling grasslands of the high Sonoran Desert near the Arizona/Mexico border, this historic hacienda serves as a reminder of the Old Southwest's gracious lifestyle. Once part of a thriving Mexican cattle operation, the ranch fell into American hands after the Gadsden Purchase of 1854. Within a few years, territorial cattle baron Colonel William Sturges began renovating and expanding the main house that subsequently became his home and the center of his ranching empire.

By the 1920s, the weathered old adobe, sheltered by a grove of towering eucalyptus trees, endured the transformation into a guest ranch christened Rancho de la Osa. Notables such as Franklin and Eleanor Roosevelt, author Margaret Mitchell, and cowboy movie star Tom Mix were guests. When a Chicago politician purchased the facility in 1935, the ranch suddenly became a political hot spot drawing Adlai Stevenson, Supreme Court Justice William O. Douglas, and Hubert Humphrey for frequent stays. William B. Clayton reportedly drafted the Marshall Plan in one of the casitas in 1948, and photographs in the library show a young Lyndon B. Johnson on horseback during a ranch visit.

Although the ranch remained a popular getaway, especially for Europeans, several of the buildings suffered neglect over the years, including a small adobe mission dating back to 1735. Finally in 1996, Richard and Veronica Schultz—drawn by the "spiritual feeling of the land"—purchased the property and began the arduous task of renovating each of the ranch's historic buildings.

"Since we wanted to return the ranch to its Mexican heritage, our first task was to scour Mexico searching for the finest antique doors, artwork, and furniture. At last count, I think we've imported

OPPOSITE: Guests convene in the dramatic dining room, part of the original hacienda dating from the 1880s. The dining table remains from the ranch's early renovation in the 1930s. RIGHT: Vivid building colors contrast with the perennial blue skies and native prickly-pear cactus. Towering eucalyptus trees shade the hacienda's courtyard.

eighteen truckloads of antiques," said Veronica. "Each building was approached as though it were a blank canvas, allowing us an unrestricted opportunity for design."

Faux finishes of richly hued tones adorn each wall, including their eighteen private casitas, and provide a backdrop for simple Mexican furnishings and colorful custom fabrics. The interiors are a sophisticated blend of hand-hewn artifacts and the Schultz's impressive contemporary art collection.

Evenings beckon their guests to the old hacienda patio for a famous ranch margarita or a sampling from their world-class wine collection. As the distinct aroma of mesquite exudes from the ranch's many fireplaces, blazing sunsets frame the vast desert vista. Nearby, under Veronica's watchful eye, the ranch chef concocts authentic southwestern cuisine encompassing a blend of Spanish, Mexican, and Native American ingredients. Herbs, lettuce, and edible flowers are cultivated in their organic garden and handpicked before each meal.

It's clear that Richard and Veronica Schultz are on a mission to preserve the heritage, flavor, and romance of Rancho de la Osa. "Our ranch has a simple elegance and a timeless serenity," says Veronica. "And we enjoy sharing it with our friends."

OPPOSITE: A series of hand-applied finishes and truckloads of Mexican antiques fill the four guest sitting rooms located in the century old building near the dining area. ABOVE: One of the larger guest sitting rooms also includes a gallery of historic photos of past ranch guests including a young Lyndon B. Johnson and John Wayne. RIGHT: Fireplaces are prominent throughout each living area. This cozy retreat features an example of Richard and Veronica's extensive painting collection.

TOP: Fabrics and furnishings reflect the ranch's western heritage in this guest casita. Rocks gathered from the surrounding desert define the fireplace. BOTTOM: When renovating the seventy-five-year-old casitas, Richard and Veronica endeavored to create a unique environment within each unit. Lighter color tones, a wood detailed ceiling and dramatic art provide an inviting refuge. OPPOSITE: Light spills across the brightly colored bedspread. In an effort to create a restful retreat, each casita features a fireplace and sitting area but no televisions or telephones.

OPPOSITE: The original pool, built in the 1920s, only lasted one season. Drifting dirt and sand quickly turned the sparkling pool into a mud bath. Today, the ranch's swimming pool is a popular gathering spot offering amazing scenic vistas. ABOVE: A small cemetery is located near an adobe mission on the ranch dating to the early 1700s. RIGHT: Design details, colors, furnishings and accessories throughout the property focus on the ranch's Mexican heritage. The old doors lead into the original ranch hacienda.

A Desert Mirage

YOU MAY HAVE SEEN Dan and Mary Trimble's home before—the custom railroad tie house has been a backdrop for a plethora of commercial ads including Nissan, Bassett Furniture, Eddie Bauer, Spiegel, AT&T, and Blue Cross/Blue Shield. Portions of Shepler's western clothing catalog have been photographed in the house, and much of the movie "Desert Snow" was filmed on location here.

While it would be easy to assume that this rustic wood cabin was set deep in the forests of the Colorado Rockies, the Trimble's secluded paradise is actually carved into the desert foothills north of Phoenix where gold claims were first staked in 1873. By the time Dan started working the land with his uncle—some fifty years ago—the gold had played out, but his family retained the mining rights and owned a sizable piece of the mountain.

In 1970, Dan and Mary set up housekeeping in a little cabin beneath the old mine and Dan started eyeing a piece of ground for his dream house. "When he brought me up here and pointed out where the house would sit, this was just a steep piece of ground with no road. But I knew Dan had a vision, so I went with it on blind faith," Mary laughed.

Dan began leveling the building site, working nights and weekends. During this time, he scoured Arizona for abandoned railroad ties. In all, Dan accumulated 600 ties that were pushed, pulled, and carried up the steep mountain grade using nothing but "brute strength."

With no building codes on the mountain, there never was a complete set of plans. Dan had a

general idea of the layout, but it changed as they continued to build. Friends helped pour the foundation and build the masonry fireplace. He hired a local electrician and plumber but erected the walls, tie by tie, himself.

"Everything I used was salvage," said Dan. "The only new lumber in the place was purchased for the roof. The house, which is about 3,500 square feet, only cost $20,000 including the appliances." After nearly five years of construction, Dan, Mary, and their son Walker, moved in.

To this day, Dan continues to build. Rock walls, patios, corrals, and additional buildings are constantly added. And though developments continue to creep up the mountain, most of their property is surrounded by state and federal land, keeping Dan and Mary secluded in their paradise mountain retreat.

OPPOSITE BOTTOM: Located near the top of the ridge, the old family gold mine was abandoned years ago. Then Dan struck another form of desert gold—water. After discovering an artesian spring, Dan built a series of cascading ponds, filled with tilapia, catfish, and koi. OPPOSITE TOP: Abandoned railroad ties gathered throughout Arizona, create the Trimble's unusual desert abode. The massive front door was hand-hewn by Dan from salvaged lumber. ABOVE: Appearing as a desert mirage, saguaro are reflected in a pool of water. UPPER RIGHT: Dan refined his stone mason skills crafting his living room fireplace from rock gathered on the property. Family memorabilia and antiques create a comfortable warm environment. BOTTOM RIGHT: Picking guitar and singing old cowboy songs around a blazing bonfire near Dan's saloon and workshop is a favorite pastime for family and friends.

The Mojave Desert

IN THE MID-1930S, thousands of desperate families from Midwestern states fled the blistering Dust Bowl and economic devastation of America's Great Depression, motoring across Route 66 to California, the land of "milk and honey." The migrants must have been overwhelmed with disappointment as they crossed into their promise land, for the harsh Mojave Desert stretched for miles before them.

This desert is a land of contrasts. Vast vistas and mile-high mountains frame volcanic cinder cones, and booming sand dunes and rock formations stand etched with messages from pre-historic residents. Many mountain ranges are nothing but bare, jagged rocks rising abruptly out of flat, sun-baked basins, sparsely covered by creosote bush and bizarrely twisted Joshua trees. Death Valley often registers the nation's hottest temperatures, and much of this desert's diversity is known only to the most intrepid explorers.

The eventual growth of this area is tied to the water of the Colorado River. This wild and raging river took millions of years to cut through the Grand Canyon, and for hundreds of years Native Americans farmed along the fertile banks of the bubbling red torrent. As the West was settled, American troops and pioneers were shuttled up and down the river on paddlewheel steamboats. Yet during the last century, a series of dams have altered the Colorado River, creating hundreds of miles of shoreline and several recreational lakes.

Downstream on the Arizona side is a most unlikely desert mirage: The London Bridge. The actual bridge that spanned the Thames River from 1824 to 1968 was shipped piece by piece from England to the Mojave Desert. This historic structure now stretches across the river to a man-made island filled with English-oriented tourist shops.

At the turn of the century, wealthy Easterners, lured by the legends of cowboys and Indians, clamored to visit the Wild West. The Santa Fe Railroad and The Fred Harvey Company teamed up to provide transportation and lodging across the territory. Young, single women known as "Harvey Girls" were recruited to work and live at the various stations along the route. Although most Harvey Houses have long been shut down, the historic Harvey House train depot in Barstow, California offers one glimpse into this area's past.

In 1926, shortly after the Santa Fe Railroad boom, another avenue of travel opened up. Over 2,400 miles of new highway, spanning nearly two-thirds of the nation from Lake Michigan in Chicago to the Pacific Ocean in Santa Monica, California linked the east to the west coast, and within a decade, a cultural icon was created. Route 66, immortalized as "The Mother Road" in John Steinbeck's *The Grapes of Wrath,* still stands as one of America's favorite western icons.

As more and more Americans took to the open road, the Mojave Desert was soon recognized as the harshest stretch of this favorite highway. The snow-capped mountains and pine forests passed near Flagstaff, Arizona were a distant memory as Route 66 meandered into the desert near Kingman, an old mining and railroad town from the 1880s. Hairpin curves and flash floods awaited travelers as they motored on toward the Colorado River, the last barrier into California. With summer temperatures topping 120 degrees, early-day migrants often crossed the desert only at night.

Because of its harsh conditions, the Mojave Desert saw little development until this century beyond mining camps and the necessary stage

OPPOSITE: An antique cart is used to enhance this Mojave desert home's charming landscape. TOP: After silent film star Clara Bow and cowboy actor Rex Ball married in 1931, they moved to the Walking Box Ranch in Searchlight, Nevada. Their sprawling Spanish-style home became a popular retreat for many Hollywood friends including Clark Gable and Lionel Barrymore. BOTTOM: Before the transatlantic railroads were complete in the 1880s, steamboats transported U.S. Army troops, passengers, and freight from San Francisco to the mouth of the Colorado River near Yuma, Arizona, and then followed the river north toward the Grand Canyon.

stops and train depots. But finally, Hoover Dam's construction in the 1930s established Boulder City, Nevada and brought new residents to the small remote town of Las Vegas, which boomed a couple decades later as a gambling Mecca. Today, thousands of modern prospectors mine the casinos of Las Vegas and Laughlin, Nevada in the comfort of air-conditioned buildings and glistening swim-ming pools. Las Vegas is currently one of the fastest growing cities in the nation.

You can experience all of these historic places by following Interstate 40 West from Flagstaff, Arizona, or by taking Interstate 15, which cuts through the Mojave Desert and winds past Las Vegas and scenic St. George, Utah.

OPPOSITE: This replica Statue of Liberty at New York, New York Hotel and Casino overlooks the nighttime activities of bustling Las Vegas. ABOVE: Instead of spanning the Thames River in England, the 900-foot infamous London Bridge was rebuilt from the shore of Lake Havasu, Arizona to a man-made island filled with unlikely English-oriented tourist shops. RIGHT: Situated on the Arizona/Nevada border, this engineering feat, originally known as the Boulder Dam, took five thousand men working 24 hours a day to complete in 1935. The Hoover Dam diverts the Colorado River water flow forming the 110-mile long Lake Mead, the largest artificial lake in the United States.

Bold and Beautiful

OPPOSITE: **By combining local and exotic woods, each with contrasting stains, functional kitchen cabinets are transformed into an architectural element. Custom niches showcase Roger's art and artifact collection.** BOTTOM: **Sheltering the front door is a sequence of walls and cooling water elements. A simple fountain hidden from the street is visible through the expansive library windows.**

IMPLE LINES. NATURAL FINISHES. Bold colors. Vivid textures. "I wanted my house to be simple and classic with an element of grandeur and always an aspect of surprise," designer Roger Thomas explained.

Grandeur and surprise—on a massive scale— is what Roger is accustomed to. As the lead designer for Las Vegas developer Steve Wynn, the designer has spent twenty years creating elaborate resort environments enjoyed by millions of visitors, including the Golden Nugget, The Mirage,

Treasure Island, and their newest creation, the elegant European-styled Bellagio. His projects have been profiled in *Architectural Digest* and international design magazines, but as Roger contemplated a new home, he envisioned a different path.

Commissioning California architect Mark Mack, Roger initiated the project with a directive: "I did not want to see out front and didn't want anyone to see inside." So with a decidedly modernist flair, Mack's resulting design is reminiscent of an old Spanish *presidio*. A sequence of colorful walls form the front façade like a fortress engaged to protect those within, and when the heavy rusted steel front door, nearly six feet wide, pivots open, a private secluded oasis is revealed.

Like a Spanish hacienda, a series of continuous rooms wrap around an inner courtyard with glass walls blending interior and exterior spaces. Although relatively large at 3700 feet, there are only a few rooms, which are separated into two wings. The two bedrooms, one for Roger's teen-aged son and a master suite, form the private wing. The public wing merges the kitchen, living room, and dining areas along with the housekeeper's quarters. Finally, a private study houses Roger's extensive collection of art books.

The walls, twelve feet high, glisten from the rich patina of brightly hued Venetian plaster. The walls seem to float since Mack incorporated a

recessed brushed aluminum base at the floor. After finishing the walls, a pattern of stained and scored self-leveling concrete floors was installed throughout the house. In the master bedroom, a radiant floor system heats the bathroom floor and continues to the bed.

Broad expanses of interior walls display a selection of Roger's contemporary art collection including two colorful portraits of Roger that were painted several years ago by his friend Andy Warhol. Custom niches with subtle back lighting feature artifacts as diverse as Dale Chihuly's hand-blown glass to prehistoric southwestern pottery. Since attaining a degree in Art History and graduating from Boston's Interlochen Arts Academy, Roger has amassed an impressive art and artifact collection and continues to acquire special pieces.

Probably the most remarkable aspect of Mack's architectural design is his use of natural light as a featured element. Deep overhangs frame each door and window opening, producing a range of shadows while protecting the interior from the harsh desert sun. A wide canopy, pierced with a large round opening, spans across the courtyard providing exterior shade throughout the day. And from dawn until dusk, light marches across the house, illuminating features that were designed to cast continually changing shadows both inside and out.

So after dwelling in his private retreat, what is Roger's favorite room? "The courtyard," he said. "Mark has perfectly integrated the desert sky as the best ceiling possible."

OPPOSITE: **Low voltage lights sparkle against the deep hue of the Venetian plastered walls in the guest bathroom, accented by an alabaster sink and built-in glass vase.** TOP: **Below Roger's fine collection of Dale Chihuly's glassworks are refigerator compartments camouflaged by the cabinetry design. Artwork sits on a metal shelf that hides a series of lighting and security control panels.** BOTTOM LEFT: **Light and shadows provide a continually changing effect.** BOTTOM RIGHT: **Hand-colored concrete floors merge into the richly hued plaster walls.**

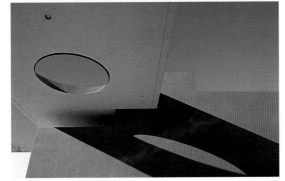

OPPOSITE: **In the library, a 300-year-old architectural artifact from the Sahara Desert region of Morocco is showcased in the ceiling.** RIGHT: **Simplicity and comfort define the master bedroom. Installing an ambient heating system in the master bathroom and along a path to the edge of the bed keeps the concrete floor comfortable even in winter. Large corner windows open onto the pool and courtyard area.**

OPPOSITE TOP: **Interior rooms with walls of windows wrap around the inner courtyard, featuring a rectangular pond filled with colorful koi. The placement and opening of the partial roof creates an ever changing canvas of light and shadows.**
OPPOSITE BOTTOM: **Light marches across the courtyard throughout the day.** ABOVE: **Hen and Chicks, a low-water-use succulent, is a popular desert landscape choice.** RIGHT: **Bold forms and colors reflect in the swimming pool visible from the master bedroom through the corner window. Rows of silver glass globes placed below blooming Redbud trees transform an ordinary space into a glistening sculpture garden.**

LEFT AND ABOVE: While stained concrete floors often feature the irregularities of a hand-produced finish, the highly polished and richly hued floors in Roger Thomas' home were achieved by staining self-leveling concrete and then applying an epoxy finish. OPPOSITE: High ceilings, softly rounded corners, and simple furnishings complement the stained concrete floors in the living room of this straw bale home.

Floors That Last a Lifetime

AN EXPOSED CONCRETE FLOOR—once limited to warehouse or industrial locations—is an increasingly popular residential choice. With today's stains, color additives, scoring, and stamping techniques, standard gray concrete can be transformed into a luxurious finish resembling marble or glazed stone.

Unlike paint, stain reacts with the minerals already present in concrete causing an uneven, variegated, and translucent color with the appearance of a time worn patina. And today, there are a myriad of color combinations.

The finishing process varies depending on the intended outcome. For consistent color, dye is mixed in with the concrete at the plant before it is installed, while acid stains are applied to the finished concrete floor for multi-hued color variations. Finally, wax or other sealants are added for an elegant polished look. In addition, concrete can be stamped to resemble stone, tile, or brick providing endless options for a customized floor.

While finished concrete floors are attractive, they are also economical, durable, and easy to maintain, requiring no harsh chemicals to clean. All you really need are a broom and a mop. A concrete floor is also a superior environmental product to carpet, vinyl, wood, or tile as there is nothing to mine, cut down, kiln dry, or synthesize, and there are no scraps or waste. Environmentally safe concrete stains are available for interior and exterior applications. (See Resources, page 160.)

Often it is difficult to finish concrete that has previously been covered with tile or carpet since the concrete surface is usually damaged. But now, a thin polymer concrete overlay, available in numerous patterns and colors, can be installed over existing surfaces making this solution viable for any home, new or old.

Concrete floors are now the perfect answer to desert design.

A Red Rock Resort

WHEN BUILDER BUD BRACKEN first met with Don and Elaine Davis to discuss building a new home, there was no way to predict the long-term friendship that would ensue. "Because they wanted me to have a thorough understanding of their taste and style, I traveled with them for three years as we researched and planned. And, of course, we became good friends," said Bud.

Don and Elaine were living in Florida at the time and as they considered future retirement, their desire was to relocate somewhere in the West. Eventually, they settled on trading their Country French lakefront home in a golf resort for the sand and sheer red cliffs of the Mojave Desert.

With a combined square footage of around 7,000 feet, the property includes the main house and a smaller casita wrapped around a resort-style courtyard. Set on a three-acre corner lot, the home is designed with numerous special amenities, including two guest suites, an exercise room, a steam shower, a customized sewing center, and an oversized two-car garage on each end. The casita is a charming one bedroom that includes a living area and a kitchen.

Bud, who spent years in the advertising business, approaches homebuilding with an unusual flair for design. Combining color and texture, he assisted in crafting the details and finishes throughout the Davis home. Natural flagstone and pine flooring blend through the living areas and provide a subtle background for area rugs. A luster and sheen reminiscent of a new car finish was achieved on the walls by applying a special pigmented plaster. Antique shutters were gathered during many trips to antique markets, and then custom openings were designed around them. And to create the smoked finish of a cozy log cabin in the family room, a gray finish was hand-rubbed into the logs.

The most unique features in the home are the wood details. The wood, taken from a train bridge that was buried under the Great Salt Lake for

over 100 years, was brought to the job site and milled into custom shelves, ceiling beams, and the family room fireplace mantle.

Family and friends are always welcome at the Davis home, so each of the guest bedrooms were thoughtfully designed with a walk-in closet, bathroom, and private patio. And in addition to the standard television, a computer with Internet access is provided in each room.

By building a double frame wall finished with stucco, the home resembles an old adobe. In some areas the walls are nearly two feet thick, providing deep windowsills. Windows and doors were strategically placed to provide cross breezes and ventilation. And in the master bedroom a private courtyard shaded by an overhang was created, always guaranteeing Don and Elaine a place to relax and read out of the desert sun.

A meandering adobe wall encloses the courtyard and is accented by the lush landscape and the soft sounds of tumbling water. Drawing on local history, the spa resembles an Indian well while a nine-foot statue stands guard over the swimming pool and waterfall. And after a summer storm, a dozen waterfalls spill over the 500 foot red rock cliffs near the Davis home. As for Don and Elaine, they've never regretted trading their lakeside golf home for this authentic red rock resort.

OPPOSITE: Granite countertops and antiqued black alder cabinets create a casual kitchen elegance accented with western accessories. Light spills in from the skylight and adjoining courtyard. ABOVE: In a departure from south-western style details, the family room is a warm replica of a log cabin. The antique white buffalo head over the fireplace was discovered at a flea market and has recently received the ceremonial blessings of nearby Native Americans.

OPPOSITE: The circular dining room features a series of clerestory windows, niches to showcase the art, and a custom dining table with a flush lazy Susan in the center. ABOVE: Coved plaster ceilings, concealed lighting, a cozy corner fireplace, and adjacent covered patios define the master bedroom. Nearby an exercise room, steam shower, and a convenient washer/dryer are part of the master suite. RIGHT: Exquisite views toward the rocky cliffs extend beyond the courtyard, swimming pool, and spa. The spa was designed to resemble an old Indian well.

A Remote Desert Oasis

ARNER AND SUSAN PAIGE are typical of many mid-westerners—as retirement approached, they wanted to leave the cold, snowy winters behind. "We explored many Southwest desert communities, but just fell in love with this area," explained Warner.

What captivated the couple was the eastern edge of the Mojave Desert near St. George, Utah. This remote area was virtually ignored by early settlers until the Morman church sent families to farm the region in 1861. And although the scenery is spectacular and the winters mild, this

OPPOSITE: **Large windows incorporating new heat shield technology wrap the living room providing stunning desert vistas. Whenever possible natural materials were selected for furnishings and finishes.**
BOTTOM: **Exterior colors are confined to selections that blend with the surrounding scenery.**

area has not seen the explosive growth like the deserts of southern Arizona and California.

Their one-and-a-half acre lot lies within the Red Cliffs Desert Preserve, which abuts the Red Mountain Wilderness and the Santa Clara River Preserve, guaranteeing their views will always be protected. Warner and Susan also recognized the professional long-term commitment of Kayenta Homes developer, Terry Marten, who twenty-five years ago established strict building codes requiring low profile, southwestern style homes and subdued lighting to protect the night skies.

"There are also restrictive covenants concerning the desert landscape," said Warner. Very little of the property's existing natural vegetation could be disturbed during construction, even the driveway and streets remain unpaved. "Many builders are intimidated by the construction constraints," said Kurt Thompson, owner of KDT Construction and the couple's builder. "But after completing several homes here, I understand the process and appreciate the end results."

Once Thompson staked out the perimeter of the Paige's home, he then staked out another perimeter less than three feet beyond the house's edge. "I had to keep all my construction within that three-foot boundary," explained the builder. "After the home was completed, I restored the three-foot construction area surrounding the house back to its natural state with native desert landscape materials."

With the same enthusiasm for creating a responsible desert habitat as his father, Matt Marten developed the Paige floor plan, creating spacious open areas defined by raising and lowering the ceilings. According to Warner, as their building plans took shape, the couple chose to "loosely follow the principals of Feng Shui," the ancient Chinese art of using color, placement, material selection, and other elements of interior design to create positive energy. Corners are rounded throughout the home and natural materials were selected wherever possible. The twelve-inch stained pine planks and flagstone flooring is accented with area rugs—no carpet was used— and butcher block and slate blend into the kitchen.

Thompson built openings to accommodate antique Spanish doors, which were discovered on numerous trips to Santa Fe. Openings are arched, utilizing grape stakes in various details, matching the grape stake *latillas* used in the ceiling's design.

Large windows wrap the living room, providing lush views of the desert and red mountains beyond. After much consideration, Warner and Susan decided not to use window coverings in this room. "We knew we didn't want draperies," explained Warner, "and all the other options we considered would have blocked parts of the windows." So in addition to the care they took in placing the house on the lot with regard to the sun, they selected high performance windows using the latest glass technology for additional sun control.

The couple chose sage green as a predominant interior color—reminiscent of the surrounding desert sage after a rain. And continuing with the

Feng Shui philosophy, furnishings and accessories were carefully selected, maintaining a simple, calming interior. For Warner and Susan Paige, this once remote section of the Mojave Desert is now their desert oasis.

OPPOSITE: **Designer Matt Marten used various ceiling and wall heights to define different areas. Details, lighting, accessories, and furnishings were kept simple and understated.** ABOVE: **A traditional arched opening beckons visitors to the Paige home, which easily blends into the dramatic red cliff landscape beyond.** RIGHT: **In the entry area flagstone floors, rounded corners, and a ceiling designed with lodgepoles and grape stakes blend southwestern style with elements of Feng Shui.**

OPPOSITE: Twelve-inch pine plank floors blend
through the spacious master suite that includes a
workout room and an office. ABOVE: This open-
air patio allows for full views of the ephemeral
waterfalls, which can be seen cascading down
the surrounding cliffs after a summer rain.

A Fireplace in the Desert?

FIREPLACES ARE LIKE COMFORT FOOD, often reminiscent of cozy, childhood memories. So while Southwest fireplaces may get less year-round use than in other parts of the country, acclimated desert dwellers still crave the crackling of a good fire when temperatures plunge on those clear, winter nights.

Credit should be given to medieval European lords for developing the fireplace as we know it today. Interior fires were completely utilitarian at that time, and they were usually located in the center of the room for heating and cooking purposes. There was no chimney; the smoke simply found its way out the cracks and openings in the ceiling above.

By the 14th century, European aristocracy, tired of smoke-filled castles, incorporated fireplaces into the wall complete with projecting hoods to capture the smoke and direct it outside. As fireplace construction improved over the next few decades, drawing most of the fire's smoke up the chimney, a decorative mantle replaced the large hood.

Today, popular styles extend beyond the Southwest's well-known kiva fireplace. Wood, stone, and faux finished cast concrete add visual interest and customizing touches. And gone are the days of stacking wood and hauling ashes. Remote control systems with gas logs provide both convenience and cleanliness. Also, many local governments are banning wood burning due to air quality concerns.

The current emphasis on energy efficiency accounts for the popular comeback of Count Rumford's 1796 fireplace. Its shallow, angled design forces more heat back into the room, and this design allows for unusually large openings, making the fireplace a dynamic focal point.

So whether it be an indoor accessory or an outdoor luxury, a fireplace is right at home in its desert surroundings.

OPPOSITE BOTTOM: This home theater showcases a modern version of a simple kiva fireplace, which features a Keltic Knot design representative of the owners' ethnic background. OPPOSITE TOP: Outdoor fireplaces extend the desert's outdoor living areas to virtually year-round use. A sculpted adobe chimney provides an inviting welcome to this protected courtyard entrance. ABOVE: Dave and Nancy Hall's rammed earth home incorporates a traditional kiva fireplace in the living room. RIGHT: This simple adobe fireplace was built in the 1880s.

A Secluded Desert Dwelling

IN 1976, AFTER COMPLETING BRIAN HEAD, southern Utah's first ski resort, architect/developer Terry Marten discovered that portions of a scenic south Utah ranch were slated to be sub-divided into five-acre trailer sites. The pristine Mojave Desert terrain included such a unique landscape that it was frequently used as the site location for numerous commercials and western movies.

After witnessing southern California's "unfortunate transformation from orange orchards to rooftops" during his childhood, Terry felt compelled to rescue the ranch from a similar fate. Within hours, he was headed to nearby St. George, Utah and ultimately purchased the entire 1,300-acre ranch bound by the Red Mountain Wilderness and the Santa Clara River Preserve. Terry dubbed the area Kayenta, meaning "water from the rocks."

Over the next decade, the developer's vision of Kayenta Homes evolved. The master plan, as unique as the land itself, designated home sites at a minimum of one-and-a-half acres with restrictions on building heights, colors, styles, and landscaping.

In the mid-1980s, the first lot was sold to Gary Collins, who was familiar with Kayenta as he'd spent considerable time in the area with his friend Robert Redford during the filming of Redford's *Jeremiah Johnson* and *The Electric Horseman.* Gary's original plans were to build a small studio, but after fifteen years, he and his wife Cheryl opted to build permanent residence on the beautiful site.

By spending nearly eighteen months in the design process, Terry, Gary, and Cheryl had plenty of time to study the land exploring ways to adapt their ideas into the sloping site. "It was a fun, collaborative effort," said Cheryl. "But even with all our planning, we still made tons of changes during construction."

Terry's passion for blending his dwellings into the terrain is evident; the new adobe home appears as though it's been there a hundred years as it rambles down the hill. "Because of restrictions limiting building heights to not more than thirteen feet, I hew the structures into the earth, which keeps a low profile from the exterior yet allows for high ceilings inside," explained Terry.

The compound ended up consisting of three parts: the main house, Gary's studio, and a guest casita. Their gracious hospitality leads to a steady stream of visitors, yet the couple wanted to maintain some personal privacy, so the master suite is secluded from the guest quarters. Most of the home's activity radiates from the unique circular kitchen lined with windows opening onto the extensive veranda and courtyard. "The house has a transparency to it," said Cheryl, "because of its design and window locations, in most areas you can stand outside and see through the house and into the landscape beyond."

Finishes and design details reflect the couple's lifestyle encompassing a blend of desert Southwest casual with the influence of grand European style gleaned from time spent at their summer home in Italy. Pigmented plaster creates an earthy aged patina. Stained concrete floors and kitchen counters are durable and easy to maintain. Each door is unique, and though they all appear old and worn, several are actually doors that were distressed, stained, and waxed to create an individual antique character.

Like many of their neighbors, due to the low-density development and strategic placement of nearby homes, the Collins' are comfortable leaving their windows free of window coverings. Special technology glass reduces the effects of the summer sun, while keeping a clear view of the surrounding

landscape. Window and door locations provide plenty of cross-breezes, reducing the need for constant air conditioning. And the home's central heat system has never been used because of consistent warmth generated from radiant heat coils installed under the concrete floors.

With their house surrounded by nearly ten acres of desert wash and protected mountainous terrain, Cheryl sums up their Kayenta home, "It feels like we live in a National Park."

ABOVE: Cheryl spent months studying the building site at various times of the day, making subtle changes to the plans as she understood how the light effected each area. An antique door discovered in Mexico opens into the courtyard.
OPPOSITE: A changing gallery of Gary's paintings are featured in the living room. With an eye for detail and design, Gary hand-selected each piece of exposed wood throughout the house.

OPPOSITE: **One of the home's most unusual features is the spacious circular kitchen wrapped with windows offering views in every direction. The stained concrete countertops were poured and finished in place.** ABOVE: **Cheryl designed several stained glass windows, which cast an array of patterns and light into various rooms.** RIGHT: **To craft a home that rambles down the sloping site, the master suite was designed off the kitchen with a step down to a lower level. A shelf over the door highlights selections of the couple's antique pottery collection.**

OPPOSITE: Typically working on several projects simultaneously from commissioned paintings to book illustrations, Gary's studio was an integral element of the overall design. ABOVE: The couple often entertains and usually dines on the large ramada off the kitchen. Vines planted along the columns will eventually produce a natural awning reminiscent of the couple's favorite Tuscany style. RIGHT: Custom lit niches with glass shelves accent the bedroom, along with antique furniture, area rugs, and gallery rails to display Gary's paintings.

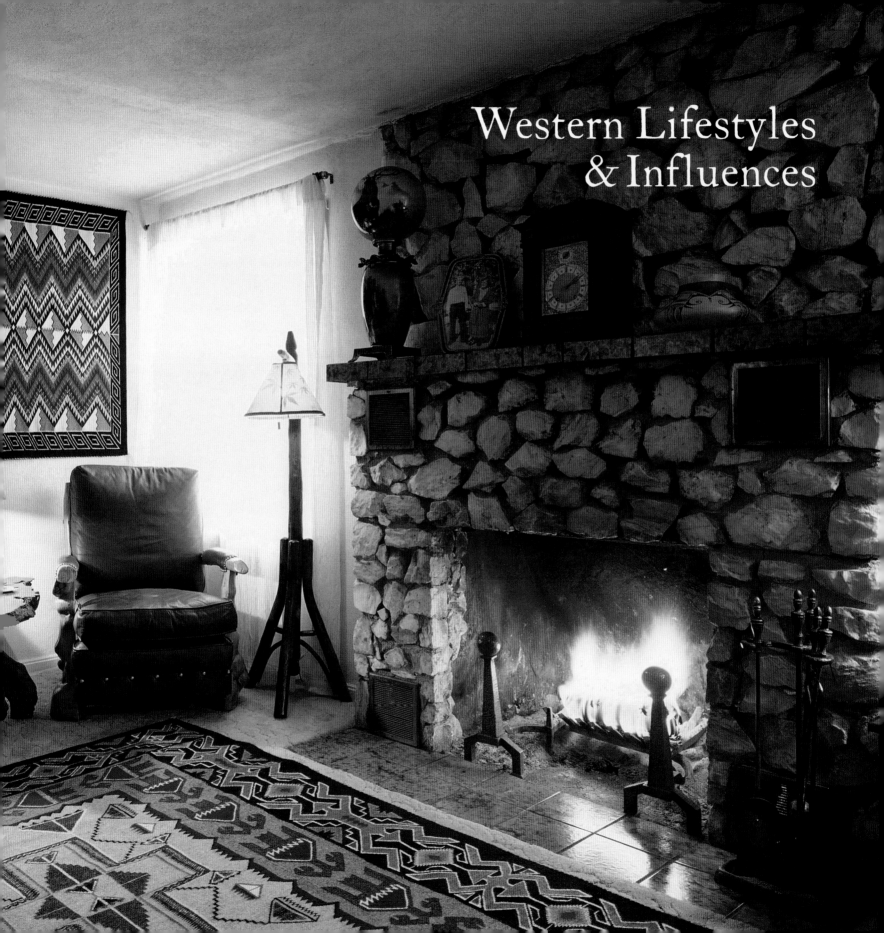

Western Lifestyles
& Influences

Legends of the West

IT'S OFTEN THE TRAPPINGS of the American West, the lore and legends of cowboys and Indians, as well as the dramatic landscape that convince unsuspecting visitors to relocate to the desert Southwest. And it's no surprise that desert natives, along with newcomers to the region, feel compelled to add a few Western Americana or Native American items to spice up their home décor.

Because America's great romance with the Old West has never waned, almost anything to do with that era in American history is considered collectible, from saddles and spurs to guns and badges. In fact, the increasing popularity has sent prices skyrocketing. A mint condition pair of 1912 custom spurs just fetched over $14,000 at a cowboy gear auction, while a spectacular parade saddle owned by Hollywood cowboy hero Roy Rogers netted more that $400,000. But if those prices are a little out of your budget, don't despair as there are plenty of western collectibles that still remain quite affordable.

To learn more about cowboy collectibles, consider contacting a collectors club such as the Cowboy Collector Network, the Cowboy Collector Society, or The National Bit, Spur, & Saddle Collectors Association. Museums are another great source of information. The Autry Museum of Western Heritage in Los Angeles, California; the Buffalo Bill Historical Center in Cody, Wyoming; and the National Cowboy & Western Heritage Museum in Oklahoma City, Oklahoma are all excellent places to visit to gather more information. (See Resources, page 160.)

Two annual cowboy collectible shows draw dealers and collectors from around the world and showcase a vast array of Old West items: High Noon's Wild West Collector's Show & Auction each January in Mesa, Arizona; and Old West Show & Auction each June in Cody, Wyoming. Reputable dealers usually offer an authenticity

OPPOSITE: **Snuff Garrett's guest bedroom blends classic ranch furniture with western fabrics. Framed historical documents line the walls.** RIGHT: **This 21 x 26" nine-color lithograph is one of a pair of posters believed to be produced for the World Columbian Exposition in Chicago, circa 1893. The pair was estimated at $14,000 to $18,000.**

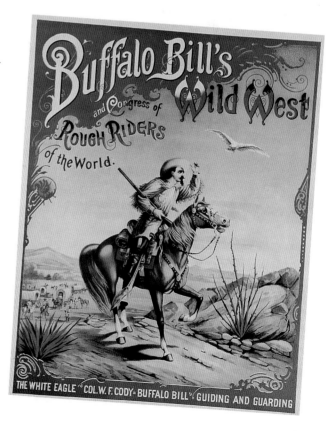

guarantee, agreeing to buy back an item if it was unintentionally misrepresented. But you should be aware of the company's policy before you procure your prized find. Just remember that age-old caveat—"buyer beware." That great pair of antique-looking rusted spurs might actually be a recent import from Mexico, and that gun, "once owned by the infamous Wyatt Earp," is probably just an empty claim. Just do a little research before you go, and you'll walk away with a genuine treasure for life.

Many residents and tourists are also eager to purchase Native American arts and crafts, either as a memento, an investment piece, or as a focal point of their home decor. The Southwest is burgeoning with galleries, artisan's shops, and full-blown tourist traps—so arm yourself with a little information before making a purchase.

The Heard Museum in Phoenix, Arizona houses one of the most extensive collections of Native American art and artifacts in the country; a great place to learn about the region's numerous native cultures. And throughout the Southwest, many local museums feature the jewelry, pottery, baskets, and weavings predominant in the area. Museum stores offer authentic merchandise and the prices are a good indication of fair market value.

With machine-made Native American reproductions coming in droves from overseas, a recently enacted law provides some consumer protection from outright fraud. The Indian Arts and Crafts Act of 1990 makes it illegal to misrepresent any arts and crafts that were produced after 1935 as "Native American-made," so always ask if an item is Native American-made. Reputable galleries often provide artist's biographies or certificates of authen-

ticity. And be wary of stores offering perpetual 50-70% discounts—if it's "too good to be true" then it is probably a reproduction.

Average prices are virtually impossible to predict because the size, quality, and condition of each hand-made item varies. For instance, Navajo weavings from 1900 to 1940 are popular collectibles; a quality 3 x 5' rug might require a $1,500-$2,000 investment. The same sized pre-1900 weaving, best suited for wall display, may run around $5000, and rarer museum quality pieces can easily range $20,000-$50,000. New weavings can be found for a few hundred dollars while reproductions are often under $100. When the PBS Antiques Roadshow came to Tucson, Arizona, a resident brought an old family rug he kept hanging on a chair. The rare mid-1800s Navajo chief's blanket received an estimated value of $350,000-$500,000.

If you'd like to purchase directly from the artist, check with local Chambers of Commerce for a schedule of art shows, usually held in the fall, winter, and spring months. Native American Fairs and Art Markets are a colorful blend of food, dancing, and art. You can also visit the many trading posts and roadside stands that dot the Southwest's Reservations. Be aware that there are different customs and regulations governing these lands. For more information, you can contact the regional Visitors Centers, which are generally located in the larger Native American communities.

Enjoy the process of acquiring your Western and Native American art and collectibles. Not only will these items enhance your interiors, but each acquisition is also a key, which opens another fascinating door into the history and culture of America's desert Southwest.

ABOVE: **A Native American boy is dressed in his rich and colorful traditional clothing.** OPPOSITE LEFT: **Custom shelves highlight this Native American pottery collection.** OPPOSITE RIGHT: **A collection of** *retablos,* **religious paintings on flat boards, hang next to colorful weavings. Weathered hand-hewn chairs flank an antique cabinet. Richly stained wood trim, irregular plaster walls, wood floors, and arched openings are elements of Spanish colonial design.**

Just Playin' Cowboy

OPPOSITE: **Snuff Garrett's office is filled with so many western historical documents and so much Hollywood movie memorabilia that he began displaying posters on the ceiling. In addition to Gene Autry's boots and shirt on the left, Roy Roger's famous double Eagle boots worn in numerous movies, a birthday gift to Snuff, are sitting on the leather chair.** BOTTOM: **In the rolling grasslands along the edge of the Chihuahuan Desert, Snuff and Nettie's horse Pecos gazes over the corral.**

S NUFF GARRETT FONDLY RECALLS WHEN, at the age of ten, he traded a prized sling shot for his friend's tattered poster—a reprint of western artist Till Goodan's colorful image of cowboys on horseback watching a plane fly over the Southwest.

"I'd just pull it out from under my bed and stare at it," said Snuff, a Texas native, who grew up spending Saturdays at the movies watching Hollywood westerns. "I wanted to be a cowboy, like Roy Rogers and Hopalong Cassidy."

But Snuff's cowboy dreams were sidelined at the early age of fourteen when he started working at a Dallas, Texas radio station. Soon his passion was music. Eventually, Snuff headed to Los Angeles, and by 1961, he'd produced his first #1 hit, Bobby Vee's "Take Good Care of My Baby." Over the next fifteen years, he rose to be one of pop music's top producers, leading Gary Lewis and the Playboys to seven straight Top Ten hits and producing three solo hits for his next door neighbor, Cher.

Even though he was living in California, Snuff never abandoned his love for the American cowboy and the Old West. After discovering another copy of the Till Goodan reprint he'd had as a child, Snuff prominently hung it in his Beverly Hills mansion amidst his impressive original art collection. A few years later, he was thrilled to come across the original Goodan painting. Today, the prized image hangs in Snuff's living room— the cornerstone of a western memorabilia collection many museums could only dream about.

Snuff eventually bought his scenic desert property in southeastern Arizona while still a California resident, splitting it with his good friend and cowboy movie legend, Rex Allen. After Snuff relocated from Los Angeles to slower-paced Paradise Valley, Arizona in the 1980s, he built a two-bedroom ranch house, which would later become Idle Spurs Ranch, as his weekend retreat.

Although simple and understated from the front, one step inside reveals an interior environment derived only through considerable planning and attention to detail, including a sunken cowboy bar

complete with cowhide barstools, a unique rock fireplace with a custom area inset specifically for Snuff's Goodan painting, hand-hewn doors, custom hardware, and a lighting system designed to highlight his extensive collections. Later, he added a master bedroom and large office, and then in 1992, Snuff moved to the remote ranch permanently.

"Ah, I'm just playin' cowboy," he laughs, but it's evident his love of the American West is serious business. The towering living room walls are filled with framed, mint condition vintage wild west and rodeo posters. A collection of antique spurs hangs over the bar. Near the vaulted ceiling, a silver-gilded saddle glistens from its custom niche, and Snuff nonchalantly mentions he once owned The Edward H. Bohlin Company—legendary producers of silver buckles, spurs, and western saddles.

Western art and sculptures, antique firearms, and historical western documents line the walls. One bathroom is filled with rodeo memorabilia, and another with a collection of colorful silk ties from Hollywood's cowboy heroes, including Snuff's old pal, "The King of the Cowboys," Roy Rogers. Roy's fancy western duds and a prized pair of his red, white, and blue cowboy boots remain among the collector's favorites. The ranch home is a walk through history from the authentic Old West to Hollywood's popularized version, and Snuff continues to acquire, trade, and sell from his vast inventory.

Any reference to Snuff's incredible success in the music business is conspicuously missing throughout the house, with just a few items relegated to a couple bookshelves in a bedroom. Although he laughs while explaining that all his gold records are collecting dust in the attic, Snuff hasn't completely abandoned the music industry, as he occasionally produces CDs filled with his favorite guitar or cowboy tunes or directs the music for special projects at the request of his Hollywood buddies Burt Reynolds and Clint Eastwood.

But after a fast-paced L.A. life, Snuff Garrett is now more than content to spend time with his wife, Nettie, and their three dogs while he's "just playin' cowboy" at their idyllic Idle Spurs Ranch.

OPPOSITE: **Above the headboard in the spacious master bedroom are five paintings by Snuff's close friend reknowned western artist Olaf Wieghorst.** ABOVE: **This guest bedroom is filled with memorabilia and artifacts from the legendary career of western movie hero Buck Jones.** RIGHT: **One step beyond the unassuming front porch and the living room ceiling soars to two-stories, filled with colorful, rare show bills and a large buffalo head dating from the 1890s. The original Till Goodan painting Snuff admired as a child hangs in its custom fireplace niche. On the table is a solid silver sombrero, an antique racing trophy.**

OPPOSITE: **To the right is Snuff's John Wayne wall featuring the actor's letters, autographed photos, and Wayne movie collectibles. Native American baskets hang over the doorway and an antler mirror is visible in the foreground. Floors are stained concrete and saguaro ribs accent the far door.** ABOVE: **Antique spurs hang above the sunken cowboy bar, and perched above are two elaborate saddles. The black saddle on the left was made by the legendary Hollywood saddlemaker Edward H. Bohlin.** RIGHT: **Snuff has more than 250 custom-made pairs of colorful cowboy boots.**

Weaving Beauty and Simplicity

OPPOSITE: **Stacks of historic and contemporary Navajo weavings fill Steve Getzwiller's office. The Germantown Chief's blanket on the wall, the gold tone, glass image from western photographer Edward Curtis, and the L&JG Stickley leather daybed are from the early 1900s.** BOTTOM: **The Getzwillers' horses graze on the grasslands.**

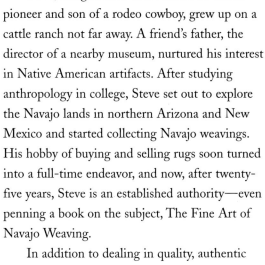

GLANCING PAST THE CANOPY OF TREES lining the winding ranch road, it's easy to understand what drew Steve and Gail Getzwiller to purchase this 70-acre horse ranch on the edge of the Chihuahuan Desert—views of the Huachuca and Whetstone Mountains to the East, the Santa Ritas to the West, and a 360 degree panoramic view from their vantage point atop a knoll in the rolling desert grasslands. But it's not just the views or the acreage for their horses and cattle, the sprawling ranch house is ideal for showcasing the Getzwillers' extensive collection of Navajo weavings and handcrafted furniture from the early 1900s American Arts & Crafts Movement.

Steve, the grandson of a Southwest desert pioneer and son of a rodeo cowboy, grew up on a cattle ranch not far away. A friend's father, the director of a nearby museum, nurtured his interest in Native American artifacts. After studying anthropology in college, Steve set out to explore the Navajo lands in northern Arizona and New Mexico and started collecting Navajo weavings. His hobby of buying and selling rugs soon turned into a full-time endeavor, and now, after twenty-five years, Steve is an established authority—even penning a book on the subject, The Fine Art of Navajo Weaving.

In addition to dealing in quality, authentic weavings, Steve's passion is reviving 19th century Navajo rug designs using wool from the nearly extinct Churro sheep. These sheep are descendants of the original herds brought to America by the Spanish in the 1700s; their long-stapled wool is ideal for weaving. After a few remaining Churro sheep were discovered in remote pockets of the Navajo Reservation in northern Arizona, Steve has worked diligently to assist in the herd's regrowth. As the Churro's numbers have increased, their sheered wool is provided to a select group of Navajo weavers, commissioned by Steve to produce highly detailed rugs that often take up to a year to complete.

About five years ago, Steve and Gail began

another quest—to find home furnishings to merge with the style of their Navajo rugs. They chose the Arts & Crafts era, or Mission-style furnishings, for their flawless designs of honesty and simplicity.

"We appreciate the philosophy behind both art forms—the inherent beauty of natural materials, simple designs, and a sense of integrity in their construction," said Gail. "The two styles complement each other perfectly." Collecting furniture like they would Navajo rugs or any other art, "by evaluating the lines, finish, and color," Steve and Gail continue to scour the country in search of original Arts & Crafts creations, often with assistance from antique dealers and auction houses, who notify the couple when new items are discovered. Luckily, their home is spacious since their furniture collection has continued to grow from tables to cabinets, and now even includes a rare desk manufactured by L&JG Stickley, Inc., one of the original companies that promoted "simple furniture built along mission lines," eventually spawning the term "Mission-style."

The Arts & Crafts furnishings blend easily with the couple's Native American pots, baskets, and other artifacts. Yet it is the colors and patterns of the Navajo rugs—some on the floor, others hanging on the walls—that define the space. But for the Getzwillers, their surroundings are often changing as they buy, sell, and trade items throughout their ranch house. "It's fun collecting and upgrading as you go along," said Steve, who's always on the lookout for that next great discovery.

OPPOSITE: The simple lines of Arts & Crafts furniture and lighting blends with the geometric designs in Navajo weavings. In the entry, both Two Grey Hills rugs date from the early 20th century as does the mission-style furniture. Steve found the circa 1910 light fixture over twenty years ago. ABOVE: On the living room floor, this 8 x 12' rug is a blaze of color and design. The intricate 4 x 9' wall hanging, produced with churro wool, took almost two years to complete and was displayed in a museum show. An original Dirk Van Erp lamp sits on the mint condition table while the rare desk features a turn-of-the-century reverse painted lamp from the Handel Lighting Company.

UPPER LEFT: This finely crafted Handel light fixture, once featured on a magazine cover, hangs over a Stickley Brothers table and chairs. Steve's uncle is in the large 1950s Ray Manley photograph taken at the last round-up on an early day Spanish land grant ranch in southern Arizona. BOTTOM LEFT: Planks of mesquite flooring in the couple's study provide a rich background for Native American weavings. Desert rocks gathered from the ranch form the fireplace while the mantle features favorite elements of the couple's collection. ABOVE: Details from the Handel chandelier. OPPOSITE: The chair on the right is a Gustav Stickley from 1904. Old Mission Copper Craft manufactured the hammered metal lamp in San Francisco around 1905. The wall hanging is a contemporary reproduction of an old Chief's blanket from Steve's Churro Collection.

Outdoor Living

WITH MONTHS OF GORGEOUS WEATHER, it's no surprise that outdoor living has been a popular component of life in the desert Southwest for centuries. Prehistoric peoples incorporated large outdoor plazas into their dwellings for socializing, trade, cooking, and ceremonies; the Spanish built their adobe homes around a central courtyard, an architectural element that continues to influence southwestern design; and American pioneers adapted quickly to the concept of outdoor living spaces, often adding elaborate flower gardens to patios and courtyards as a reminder of life back East.

By the mid-1950s, technology brought swimming pools, covered patios, and the barbeque grill. Along with a couple lounge chairs and a patio table, the modern backyard was complete. But often these outdoor spaces were used sporadically, avoided on chilly winter evenings or hot summer days, and rarely were they considered an extension of the home's design.

Today, with proper planning, the desert home expands into a series of outdoor living areas comfortable by day or night and enjoyed year round. As the popularity of indoor/outdoor space escalates, design professionals seek new building products to improve the efficiency and effectiveness of these blended areas. Elements prevalent for decades, like the outdoor fireplace, are enhanced. Many homes are now designed with a variety of fireplaces strategically placed throughout outdoor living areas. Often the focal point of the outdoor living room, full-sized fireplaces complete with hearth and mantle provide that perfect cozy spot to watch a winter sunset. Then instead of retreating to the confines of air conditioning in the heat of the summer, a well-placed misting system along a covered patio cools the dry air and creates a welcome respite from the desert sun.

Outdoor living areas are approached with the same thought and design as any interior space. In addition to maintaining a visual flow of styles, colors, and finishes, exterior lighting creates dramatic nighttime spaces, illuminating the architecture

and landscape for dusk to dawn enjoyment. Moods are defined by concealing the light source. Underwater low voltage lights cast a shimmering hue. Pathway lighting, flush to the ground, is a sensitive alternative to the overpowering flood-light. And where desert communities have outdoor lighting restrictions to protect the night skies, subtle low-level lighting is a necessity.

Since desert dwellers enjoy months of outdoor cooking and dining, complete outdoor kitchens have become a favorite amenity. While the outdoor grill is still the heart of any cookout, patio kitchens typically include a cooktop, sink, and refrigerator, plus plenty of counterspace, cabinets, and storage, eliminating constant trips back and forth to the house. And because baking inside during the summer is often avoided due to the oven's residual heat, an outdoor pizza oven is also popular. Other practical options include an undercounter icemaker and residential water fountain.

And last but definitely not least, much of the desert's outdoor lifestyle revolves around the swimming pool. Once a rectangular concrete hole, the swimming pool has evolved into a customized water oasis with seemingly endless options and features. Rock waterfalls, soothing spas, elaborate fountains, lap pools, diving pools, and play pools are just a fraction of the design choices. And by simply adding a heating system, swimming in the desert is possible year round.

Unlike the prehistoric southwestern people who spent much of their time outside by necessity, modern desert dwellers are spending more time living outdoors by choice. Merging technology with design, today's desert home is a creative, yet efficient blend of indoor and outdoor environments.

PREVIOUS PAGE: **Today's desert home blends exterior and interior living areas, which are comfortable by day or night and enjoyed year round.** OPPOSITE TOP: **A blaze of flowers accents the patio of this charming Spanish home built in the 1920s.** OPPOSITE BOTTOM: **The late designer Bill Tull created this dramatic outdoor fireplace amidst the natural boulders north of Phoenix, Arizona.** RIGHT: **A thick covering of vines shelters this spacious outdoor living area offering a comfortable haven for dining or relaxing by the fire.**

OPPOSITE: **Convenience tops the list of reasons outdoor kitchens have surged. In addition to the typical outdoor grill, other favorite amenities include a sink, undercounter refrigerator, pizza oven, and a drinking fountain.** ABOVE: **Nestled in the mountains overlooking Phoenix, Arizona, this Frank Lloyd Wright style home features an infinity-edge swimming pool and expansive valley views.** RIGHT: **A rambling adobe wall meanders along the rugged Sonoran Desert terrain. Water spills through the boulders into the spa, a perfect spot to watch a blazing desert sunset.**

OPPOSITE: **Reflected in this elliptical infinity-edge pool is the rammed earth, glass, and steel home of Phoenix architect Eddie Jones. The 18 x 40' glass wall provides uninterrupted views of the Phoenix South Mountain Preserve.** ABOVE: **Handcrafted chairs blend into the natural landscape, creating a favorite outdoor space for friends and family to gather.** RIGHT: **When architect William F. Cody designed his Palm Springs modernist home, he stretched the indoor/outdoor living philosophy by incorporating an exterior shower.**

A Desert Metamorphosis

OPPOSITE: **Palo verde and ironwood trees provide a canopy of shade over the crushed granite trails meandering through the property. A simple bench offers an ideal refuge for reading or contemplation.** BOTTOM: **The home's enclosed entry, transformed to an open flagstone patio shaded by a wooden trellis, is now a favorite spot to sip morning coffee or watch the desert's summer storms roll in.**

WHEN LANDSCAPE ARCHITECT Christine Ten Eyck was first approached to renovate this urban one-acre property, the owners had a few goals in mind. Since their children, who were young when they had moved into the house, were now grown, they wanted to blend the indoor/outdoor spaces of the house while creating additional outdoor gathering areas and garden spaces.

Even though this home is located in the heart of the city, it is tucked back on a narrow street in a quaint neighborhood with a distinct feeling of being in the country. A large circular driveway dominated the front of the house while across the vast back-yard, a sizeable swimming pool was surrounded by a carpet of grass and flanked by mature grapefruit, orange, and lemon trees. Hidden behind the wall of citrus trees was another open play area popular in years past for school parties and scout campouts.

As Christine formulated her design, she focused on the front and almost immediately knew one thing for certain, the asphalt drive that consumed the front yard had to go. "I felt this area should be a garden, not a parking lot," said Christine. And even though the couple was a bit skeptical at first, now they can't imagine their landscape any other way.

To deal with the necessary driveway and space for guests' cars, the drive was rerouted on the outskirts of the property leading straight to the garage with a hidden parking bay for visitors. And instead of the typical asphalt or concrete drive, crushed granite merges with the surrounding desert terrain. With their cars sheltered from view, visitors follow a meandering desert trail toward the home's prominent new entry.

The owners wanted to enjoy the entire property, so an existing small entry area in the front was transformed into an inviting flagstone patio opening out onto their new lush desert landscape. By incorporating an open wood trellis-style overhang, portions of the summer sun are blocked while shafts of winter light offer a delightful spot for morning coffee.

Because the backyard retains the large grassy lawn and park-like ambiance, flowerbeds blend a mix of colorful annuals and perennials, offering a distinctive change from the front's desertscape. Plants soften the space between the backyard patio and pool while nearby a simple curved wall was added, defining an intimate corner patio. With thoughtful planning, visions of colorful iris, geraniums, and snapdragons are equally enjoyable from inside through a large bay window or from the outdoor patios.

In keeping with the owners' desire for shade and a sense of serenity, mature desert trees were strategically placed creating a canopy of light and shadows along the series of winding trails. To visually seclude the home, shade-tolerant hummingbird plants were mingled with the trees along the street's edge. Wildflowers produce a blaze of color and fragrance amidst the cactus and boulders discovered along the trails.

With the home now virtually invisible from the street, the owners are thankful they made this grand change. They can now sit back, relax, and enjoy their peaceful, serene desert garden.

OPPOSITE AND RIGHT: **Designed** to reflect the
ambiance of a desert trail, several pathways lead
from the street, driveway, and hidden visitor
parking bay to the front patio entrance. Along the
trails, large boulders, native cactus, and flowering
desert plants create a surprise around every
bend. During the springtime, the yard blazes
with brilliant hues of desert flowers.

ABOVE: **(After) The remarkable transformation
from a typical residential front yard to a lush
desert park is illustrated by this view towards the
front patio.** LEFT: **(Before) Originally, the front
yard was a sea of asphalt and grass.** OPPOSITE:
**Landscape architect Christine Ten Eyck's goal
was simple. "I wanted to create a space where
city dwellers could enjoy the desert."**

Xeriscape: Dry Vistas

XERISCAPE IS A LANDSCAPE METHOD based on water conservation principles that can be applied to every garden style from traditional English, formal Japanese, to natural desert landscaping. The word xeriscape is derived from the Greek word xeros meaning "dry" and the English word scape meaning "vista or view."

The concept of "water conservation through creative and appropriate landscaping" is gaining momentum throughout the country, but it's particularly important in the rain-starved desert Southwest, where water thirsty plants from other regions have been popular landscape choices over the last century. By utilizing the principles of xeriscape, a colorful, lush, and vivid garden oasis is possible while using our natural resources wisely.

With nearly 50 percent of household water consumption attributed to landscape maintenance, many southwestern communities now mandate desert landscaping in new developments. For "do-it-yourselfers," xeriscape classes are available through local water departments, and numerous books profile the thousands of plants suitable for various desert climate zones. Local plant nurseries and demonstration gardens (see Resources, page 160) display native plants and offer practical landscape methods. Experienced landscape professionals often save homeowners time and money with creative designs specifying appropriate plant materials and irrigation systems.

The seven principles of xeriscape were established nearly two decades ago by a Denver, Colorado task force studying water conservation. Planning and design, soil improvement, appropriate plant selection, practical turf areas, efficient irrigation, use of mulches, and appropriate maintenance are all elements of traditional landscaping, but it is the combination of all seven principles that results in a water-wise attractive landscape.

First, a well-researched plan is the most critical step of a successful xeriscape design. The oasis zone or areas of activity such as the patio, entryway, play area, etc. are typically the most colorful and require more water. Zones then transition to moderate and infrequent irrigation needs.

Proper soil preparation, the second principle, improves root development and allows for better water penetration. So before installing any plants or an irrigation system, a soil analysis by a university extension center or a local nursery is imperative.

The third and most enjoyable principle of xeriscape involves selecting the appropriate plants. Today's wide variety of water-efficient plant materials provides limitless landscape choices from year-round greenery, fragrant bright flowers, ground covers, trees, vines, and borders. Many nurseries even tag their low-water-use plants for easy identification.

The fourth and most misunderstood concept of xeriscape is the appropriate use of turf grasses. Lawns provide play areas and often act as a cooling element but it is still the thirstiest component of any landscape. When not needed for recreation purposes, ground covers can replace extensive turf areas. A large variety of hardy grasses and ground covers are available for different desert climates.

An efficient irrigation system is the next integral part of landscape planning. By grouping similar water-use plants, irrigation is possible with little or no water waste. Using landscape mulch, the sixth principle, from shredded bark to colored rock, enhances the design, cools the soil, and prevents evaporation. And finally, while any landscape requires periodic maintenance, the time and cost is typically reduced in a properly designed xeriscape garden.

ABOVE AND OPPOSITE: **By utilizing the principles of xeriscape, a colorful, lush, and vivid garden oasis is possible while using our natural resources wisely. A wide variety of native desert plants are available at local gardening centers. See Resources, page 160.**

From Rugged to Remarkable

ONCE INSIDE THE PROTECTIVE ADOBE WALLS, this lush desert retreat appears to be far from the noise and intrusion of city life. In fact, the 4.5-acre compound sits in the middle of central Phoenix, whose sprawling area now includes more than 3 million people. But with the skill and tenacity of landscape architect Christine Ten Eyck, this sheltered oasis embodies all the traditional elements of Southwest style and desert living.

The compound's three adobe buildings were built in the 1920s, when the initial wave of winter weary Easterners discovered the desert's glorious weather. But in the decades since its completion, the buildings and surrounding landscape fell into disrepair. Christine, along with a local architect and interior designer, was challenged with the creative task of not only returning the compound to its original simple splendor, but also incorporating modern elements in a sensitive, subtle manner.

"Our goal was to create a series of outdoor rooms in the spaces between the buildings," said Christine. "I wanted the gardens and outdoor living areas to complement the architecture's hand-crafted beauty and simplicity."

Crushed granite, chosen to blend with the desert earth, forms a narrow winding trail leading past existing prickly pear, saguaro, and creosote bushes to the secluded buildings tucked onto the corner of the property. In an effort to "intensify the desert," a variety of native flowering shrubs and desert wildflowers were added that naturally blended into the terrain.

Upon arrival at the exterior gates, the lacy limbs of numerous mature desert trees create a canopy of light and shadows, shading the large central courtyard. In a quest for the character and shade only provided by mature trees, several full-sized specimens were salvaged and once installed, appeared as though they had been there for years. It took a crane to lift each crated tree over the outside wall and gently set it into place.

Various patios were built offering an option of outdoor entertainment settings from large gatherings on the center patio to an intimate dinner party near the new swimming pool. By working within the confines of existing vegetation, the pool is surrounded by colorful native shrubs, enhancing the feeling of swimming in a desert meadow.

So with the quiet splash of the courtyard's fountain blended with the visual eloquence of desert wildflowers, this secluded adobe compound went from the most rugged desert terrain to a remarkable outdoor environment.

OPPOSITE: **Rambling along the property's front acreage, the crushed granite driveway is virtually camouflaged in the cactus and native desert plants incorporated along the narrow road.** ABOVE: **(After) Mature native trees, salvaged from demolition, blend with flowering desert plants near the renovated adobe dwellings, where a series of outdoor living areas were created.** RIGHT: **(Before) The aged buildings were in various stages of disrepair and the landscape in this area was barren.**

ABOVE: **(After) Soothing sounds of water create a favorite outdoor living area. Notice the mature trees on either side of the fountain. These salvaged specimens had to be crated in enormous boxes and lowered into place by a crane.** LEFT: **(Before) This old fountain area was in drastic need of repair.** OPPOSITE: **Without sacrificing the** mature existing saguaro and prickly-pear cactus, a new swimming pool was tucked into the area incorporating a simple narrow pool edge. By adding colorful wildflowers and blooming native plants, it gives the feeling of swimming within a desert meadow.

Life in the Great Outdoors

MAYBE THE MOST CHARMING ELEMENT of Southwest design is the blending of courtyards, fountains, and gardens within the various styles of today's desert homes. It has become a favorite place, a place where patios and courtyards merge house and garden—a room without a ceiling.

Patios have typically been located on the back of the house, often just a slab of concrete. With some planning, even a modest amount of effort can transform a simple patio into an inviting outdoor living area. Flagstone, brick, and Mexican tile are popular, durable flooring choices. Consider expanding the patio's size to incorporate a dining area and seating space as long as it stays in proportion with the house. Surrounding the patio with a short wall and iron gate adds a detailed custom appearance. And desert patios should have some sort of overhang or covering as a protective shield from the sun. Welcoming entry patios and courtyards, perhaps reminiscent of the old front porch, are also popular.

From cascading water to shooting streams, fountains are a focal point of any outdoor space. While flowing water is tranquil, the sound also masks unwanted noise such as nearby road traffic. Fountain designs are virtually endless but should be planned in conjunction with the home's architecture and outdoor landscaping. With proper exterior lighting, fountains can be enjoyed any time of the day or night. On average, a 500-square-foot fountain uses around 1,500 gallons of water per month compared to approximately 50,000 gallons required to maintain a lawn.

Gardeners love the desert's year round growing seasons. Containers and flowerbeds blaze with vivid desert blossoms and accent plants. Citrus and nut trees, burgeoning vegetable gardens, and especially roses thrive in the desert environment. With some research and planning, butterflies and hummingbirds flock to desert flora adding yet another dimension to garden life. By blending the unique textures, forms, and colors of the area's native cactus, gardens reflect the casual spirit of the desert. And with a few embellishments—a bench tucked under a tree, arbors and trellises laced with blooming vines, birds splashing in a bath, colorful koi lazily swimming in a small pond—even an ordinary backyard becomes a living work of art.

Gardens and outdoor spaces evolve over time, and the work and patience are well worth the wait. When desert dwellers are asked about their favorite room in the house, they most frequently reply, "My favorite room is outdoors."

OPPOSITE TOP: **This desert patio incorporates a simple adobe brick wall and bench along with crushed rock and a xeriscaped garden.** OPPOSITE BOTTOM: **Reflections of the mountains and rugged terrain into an infinity-edge pool blur the line between water and desert.** ABOVE: **Fountains remain a popular element of outdoor living.** UPPER RIGHT: **A steep-sloping site inspired the creation of this desert garden and the rock-lined swimming pool.** BOTTOM RIGHT: **Expansive desert vistas and blazing sunsets add to the enjoyment of this desert outdoor living area.**

Acknowledgements

AS I REFLECT on the process of writing *The Desert Home*, I recognize that this project could not have been accomplished without the contributions and assistance of many people. First, I'd like to thank the homeowners profiled on the following pages for opening their private dwellings to us— their homes truly convey the essence of real desert living. I'd also like to offer a gracious "thank you" to the talented professional interior designers, architects, and landscape architects who provided invaluable information and photographs of their desert projects. I was continually amazed at their innovative design solutions and commitment to the desert lifestyle.

In working with photographer Terry Moore over the last few months, I gleaned a newfound respect for the light, shadows, and sculptural ambiance of our southwestern deserts. And while Terry provided much of the book's photography, I can't overlook the artistic vision of the other professional photographers featured within these pages who also captured the details of desert design.

I would also like to thank a few special folks for their "behind the scenes" support. Because of Mary Ann Dobson, I gained an insightful view of El Paso's history and architecture. Bob Skolnick, publisher of *Ventanas del Valle,* and his assistant, Beth Farris, graciously supplied source materials and contacts from their southern New Mexico magazine. In Palm Springs, Jeff Hocker blended a research trip with a glimpse into the lifestyles of the "rich and famous." And thanks to Peter Brooks, owner of Palm Springs Rental Agency, for his hospitality and for arranging an entrée into several of the featured modernist homes.

Thank you to Baxter and Cindy Black, along with Teddie and Tommy Thomson, who offered a restful respite to the highway motel as I criss-crossed the desert regions; and to the dozens of people from museums, state tourism offices, and local historical agencies who assisted in my research by providing historical and local photographs.

Thanks to my Editor, Tammy Gales, for her patience in leading me through each deadline as this project progressed. And thank you to Northland's Publisher, David Jenney, for his creative ability to direct this book from conception to completion.

On a personal note, I would like to offer a deep-felt gratitude to my parents, Guy and Phyllis Logsdon who surrounded my sisters and me with a home filled with music and books. And to Audra, I appreciate your endless support.

Finally, I would like to give a huge "thank you" to Jim and our children Grace, Will, and Sam, who had to live with their mom's unpredictable writing schedule. As major deadlines approached, they knew I might be "missing in action" for hours or days at a time. Thanks for setting a place for me at the dinner table even when you knew I might not be there.

Resources

Architects, Designers, Builders, & Landscape Architects

American Society of Interior Designers
www.asid.org

American Institute of Architects
www.aia.org

American Institute of Landscape Architects
www.asla.org

Bracken Custom Homes
Bud Bracken
476 Riverside Drive
St. George, UT 85770
(435) 673-8490
www.brackencustomhomes.com

CCBG Architects, Inc.
Joe Groff, Architect
818 N. 1st Street
Phoenix, AZ 85004
(602) 258-2211
www.ccbg-arch.com

Design & Building Consultants, Inc.
Paul Weiner, Architect
19 E. 15th Street
Tucson, AZ 85701
(520) 792-0873

Est Est, Inc.
Tony Sutton, Interior Designer
17770 N. Pacesetter Way
Scottsdale, AZ 85255
(480) 563-1555
www.estestinc.com

Ford, Powell, & Carson
Chris Carson, Architect
1138 E. Commerce Street
San Antonio, TX 78205
(210) 226-1246
www.fpcarch.com

Roberts Jones Associates Architects
2525 E. Arizona Biltmore Circle, Ste. 237
Phoenix, AZ 85006
(602) 955-7575
www.robertsjones.com

Jones Studio, Inc.
Architecture & Environmental Design
4450 N. 12th Street, Ste. 104
Phoenix, AZ 85014
(602) 264-2941
www.jonesstudioinc.com

KDT Construction, Inc.
Kurt Thompson
P.O. Box 1143
Santa Clara, UT 84765
(435) 628-8159
www.kdtconstruction.com

Kayenta Homesites, Inc.
Terry Marten, Developer
800 N. Kayenta Parkway
Ivins, UT 84738
(435) 628-7234
www.kayentahomes.com

M A C K Architects
Mark Mack, Architect
2343 Eastern Court
Venice, CA 90291
(310) 822-0094
www.markmack.com

Rammed Earth Development
Tom Wuelpern
265 W. 18th Street
Tucson, AZ 85701
(520) 623-2784
www.rammedearth.com

Rammed Earth Solar Homes, Inc.
Quentin Branch
1232 E. Linden Street
Tucson, AZ 85719
(520) 623-6889
www.rammedearthhomes.com

Rod Rasmussen Landscaping
2 W. St. George Blvd., #30
St. George, UT 84770
(435) 467-8700

Robinson & Shades Design Group
Linda Robinson, Interior Designer
2700 N. Campbell Ave., Ste. 200
Tucson, AZ 85719
(520) 326-2445

Soledad Canyon Earth Builders
Mario and Pat Bellestri
949 S. Melendres Street
Las Cruces, NM 88005
(505) 527-9897
www.adobe-home.com

Sonoran Desert Designs, Inc.
Phil Hebets, Landscape Designer
31055 N. 56th Street
Cave Creek, AZ 85331
(480) 595-6400
www.sonorandesertdesigns.com

Stenjem Builders, Inc.
Eldon Stenjem
7551 N. San Manuel Road
Scottsdale, AZ 85258
(480) 998-8761

Ten Eyck Landscape Architects
Christine Ten Eyck, Landscape Architect
3807 N. 24th Street, #100
Phoenix, AZ 85016
(602) 468-0505

Donald A. Wexler, AIA
WWCOT
199 S. Civic Drive, Ste. 10
Palm Springs, CA 92262
(760) 320-1709
www.wwcot.com

Building Materials & Resources

C&D Southwest Lumber Corp.
500 N. 17th Street
Las Cruces, NM 88005
(505) 526-2131
www.zianet.com/cdlumber
Cedar vigas, latillas, and corbels.

Cantera Doors
8295 E. Raintree Drive, Ste. F
Scottsdale, Arizona 85260
(480) 367-0944
6737 E. Camino Principal, Ste. E
Tucson, AZ 85715
(520) 546-8452
6380 S. Valley View Blvd., Ste. 300
Las Vegas, NV 89118
(702) 914-2238
www.canteradoors.com
Hand-forged iron doors, handles, lamps, and gates.

Clay Mine Adobe
6401 W. Old Ajo Way
Tucson , AZ 85753
(505) 578-2222
www.claymineadobe.com
Stabilized adobe bricks.

DAWN Southwest
6570 W. Illinois
Tucson, AZ 85735
(520) 624-1673
www.greenbuilder.com/dawn
Consulting, workshops, and mail-order materials on sustainable building.

Ebeniste
2972 S. Rainbow, Ste. B
Las Vegas, NV 89146
(702) 368-2280
Custom cabinetry and closet design.

Enchanted Gardens
413 Griggs Street
Las Cruces, NM 88005
(505) 524-1886

www.nmenchantedgardens.com
Native plants, gardening tools, books, and classes.

Hopper Finishes
302 S. 30th Street
Phoenix, AZ 85034
(602) 273-1338
www.hopperfinishes.com
Specialty pigmented plasters for an old-world aged patina.

Illumination
7336 E. Shoeman Lane, Ste. 107
Scottsdale, AZ 85251
(480) 663-1200
www.illuminationdesigners.com
Professional outdoor lighting designers.

Mesilla Woodworks
1802 Avenida de Mesilla
Las Cruces, NM 88005
(505) 523-1362
Southwestern style doors, cabinets, and furniture available from the showroom or custom order.

Mexican Tile Company
2222 E. Thomas Road
Phoenix, AZ 85016
(602) 954-6271
1148 E. Broadway
Tucson, AZ 85719
(520) 622-4320
Imported Mexican tile, pavers, and sinks.

Old Pueblo Adobe Company
9353 N. Casa Grande Highway
Tucson, AZ 85743
(800) 327-4705
www.oldpuebloadobe.com
Adobe bricks, hand-peeled vigas and latillas, ocotillo fencing, hand-hewn timbers, and corbels.

Scottsdale Design Center
15125 N. Hayden Road
Scottsdale, AZ 85260
(480) 991-8247
www.scottsdaledesigncenter.com
Numerous design showrooms open to the public featuring building products, furnishings, and accessories.

Southwest Door Company
9280 E. Old Vail Road
Tucson, AZ 85747
(520) 574-7374
www.southwest-door.com
Pine, cedar, and mesquite doors, cabinet fronts, and flooring.

Sueños Antiguos Architectural Products, Inc.
801 E. Seventh Street
Tucson, AZ 85719
(520) 882-4584
Imported Mexican pavers, architectural elements, and planters.

Bill and Athena Steen
HC1 Box 324
Elgin, AZ 85611
(520) 455-5548
www.caneloproject.com
Straw bale workshops.

Texas Green Builder Association
www.greenbuilder.com

Torres Welding
P.O. Box 383
Fairacres, NM 88033
(505) 526-1648
torresweld@zianet.com
Ornamental iron staircases and gates.

Furnishings, Accessories, & Galleries

Antigua de Mexico
3235 W. Orange Grove Road
Tucson, AZ 85740
(520) 742-7114
www.mexicanmart.com
Imported items from Mexico and South America.

Bandini Johnson Gallery
760 N. Palm Canyon Drive
Palm Springs, CA 92262
(760) 323-7805
Features vintage barware, serveware, lamps, and accessories from the 1920s to the present.

Bates Collection
7034 Main Street
Scottsdale, AZ 85251
(480) 970-3025
www.batesarchitectural.com
Antique colonial furniture, doors, stone elements, religious artifacts, and accessories.

Datura Gallery
845 Coyote Gulch Court
Ivins, UT 84738
(435) 674-9595
Original fine art, custom jewelry, metalwork, fused glass, and pottery.

El Paseo Gallery
73-425 El Paseo
Palm Desert, CA 92260
(866) 357-2736
www.elpaseogallery.com
Features western and Native American art.

Ernest Thompson Furniture
7111 E. Tierra Buena Ln., Ste. 100
Scottsdale, AZ 85254
(480) 905-0727
www.ernestthompson.com
Spanish colonial and Mission hand-crafted furnishings. Also, Sombraje twig shutters, doors, and cabinets.

Fiesta Furnishings
15320 N. Hayden Road
Scottsdale, AZ 85260
(480) 951-3239
Large showroom of distinctive hand-crafted furnishings including mesquite furniture, custom upholstery, and accessories.

Galeria San Ysidro
801 Texas Avenue
El Paso, TX 79901
(915) 544-4444
www.galeriasanysidro.com
Antique architectural elements and decorative arts imported from Mexico, Spain, Northern Africa, etc. Also, custom ironwork, furnishings, and lighting.

Glenn Cutter Gallery
2640 El Paseo Road
Las Cruces, NM 88001
(505) 524-4300
Paintings, sculpture, custom jewelry, and decorative accessories.

Holler and Sanders, Ltd.
P.O. Box 2151
Nogales, AZ 85268
(520) 287-5153
Antiques, architectural items, pottery, and stoneware. By appointment only.

Hurd-La Rinconada Gallery
P.O. Box 100
San Patricio, NM 88348
www.wyethartists.com
Features paintings from three generations of the prominent Wyeth/Hurd family at Peter Hurd's historic Sentinel Ranch.

The Modern Way
1426 N. Palm Canyon Drive
Palm Springs, CA 92262
(760) 320-5455
Vintage mid-century furniture and accessories from the 1940s-70s.

Perry/Fuld Design & Manufacturing
276 S. Park Avenue
Tucson, AZ 85719
(800) 880-5152
Custom metal furnishings, drapery, and door hardware.

Ryan Gallery
2972 S. Rainbow, Ste. A
Las Vegas, NV 89146
(702) 368-0545
Original artwork, fine crafts, sculpture, and custom framing.

Sage Outdoor Decor
2 W. St. George Blvd., #30
St. George, UT 84770
(435) 628-8700
Unique outdoor furniture, garden accessories, and garden gifts.

**Scottsdale's Main Street
Art District**
Scottsdale, AZ
(480) 990-3939
www.scottsdalegalleries.com
Numerous world-renowned western and Native American galleries.

Steve Getzwiller's Amerind Art
P.O. Box 36
Benson, AZ 85602
(520) 586-2579
www.navajorug.com
Contemporary and historic Navajo weavings and other select Native American art. By appointment only.

Tejas Trading Company
446 W. 100th South
St. George, UT 84770
(435) 673-5700
www.tejastradingcompany.com
Western and Native American art and collectibles.

Waddell Trading Co.
Tempe, AZ
(480) 755-8080
Collector quality Native American arts dealer. Features kachinas, pottery, and jewelry. By appointment only.

Historic Desert Accomodations

Cibolo Creek Ranch
P.O. Box 44
Shafter, TX 79850
(915) 229-3737
www.cibolocreekranch.com

Hurd Ranch Guest Homes
P.O. Box 100
San Patricio, NM 88348
(800) 658-6912
www.wyethartists.com

Rancho de la Osa
P.O. Box 1
Sasabe, AZ 85633
(800) 872-6240
www.ranchodelaosa.com

Desert Demonstration Gardens

Arizona-Sonoran Desert Museum
2021 N. Kinney Road
Tucson, AZ 85743
(520) 883-1380
A zoo, natural history museum, and botanical garden featuring the flora and fauna of the Sonoran Desert.

Chihuahuan Desert Gardens
UTEP Centennial Museum
El Paso, TX 79968
(915) 747-5565
Extensive series of gardens show-casing plants, native stone walls, and other natural materials found in the Chihuahuan desert.

Desert Botanical Gardens
1201 N. Galvin Parkway
Phoenix, AZ 85008
(480) 941-1217
20,000 plants from deserts around the world.

Desert Demonstration Gardens
3701 W. Alta Drive
Las Vegas, NV 89153
(702) 258-3205
Theme gardens with over 1,000 species native to the Mojave Desert.

Moorten Botanical Garden
1701 S. Palm Canyon Drive
Palm Springs, CA 92264
(760) 327-6555
Living museum featuring 3,000 varieties of cacti, succulents, and desert flowers.

Water Conservation Garden
12122 Cuyamaca College Dr.
West
El Cajon, CA 92019
(619) 660-0614
The seven principles of xeriscape are introduced through a series of water saving gardening techniques.

Western and Native American Museums, Clubs, & Shows

**Autry Museum of
Western Heritage**
4700 Western Heritage Way
Los Angeles, CA 90027
(323) 667-0988
www.autry-museum.org

Buffalo Bill Historical Center
720 Sheridan Ave.
Cody, WY 82414
(307) 587-4771
www.bbhc.org

**Cowboy Artists of America
Museum**
1550 Bandera Highway
Kerrville, TX 78029
(830) 896-2553
www.caamuseum.com

Cowboy Collector Network
(714) 840-3942
www.hopalong.com

Cowboy Collector Society
(800) 327-6923

Gilcrease Museum
1400 N. Gilcrease Road
Tulsa, OK 74127
(918) 596-2700
www.gilcrease.org

Heard Museum
2301 N. Central Avenue
Phoenix, AZ 85004
(602) 252-8848
www.heard.org

**High Noon's Wild West
Collector's Show & Auction**
Mesa, AZ
(310) 202-9010
www.highnoon.com

**The National Bit, Spur, & Saddle
Collectors Association**
(520) 876-0492

**National Cowboy & Western
Heritage Museum**
1700 N.E. 63rd Street
Oklahoma City, OK 73111
(405) 478-2250
www.nationalcowboymuseum.org

**National Cowgirl Museum
and Hall of Fame**
1720 Gendy Street
Fort Worth, TX 76107
(817) 336-4475
www.cowgirl.net

Old West Show & Auction
Cody, WY
(307) 587-9014
www.codyoldwest.com

**The Roy Rogers-
Dale Evans Museum**
15650 Seneca Road
Victorville, CA 92392
(760) 243-4547
www.royrogers.com

Bibliography

Abbey, Edward. *Desert Solitaire: A Season in the Wilderness.* New York: Simon & Schuster, 1990. (This book was first copyrighted by Edward Abbey in 1968.)

Baker, John Milnes. *American House Styles: A Concise Guide.* New York: W.W. Lorton & Company, Inc., 1994.

Burba, Nora & Panich, Paula. *The Desert Southwest.* New York: Bantam Books, 1987.

Cohan, Tony. *Mexicolor; The Spirit of Mexican Design.* San Francisco: Chronicle Books, 1998.

Cygelman, Adele. *Palm Springs Modern: Houses in the California Desert.* New York: Rizzoli Publications, Inc., 1999.

Easton, David. *The Rammed Earth House.* White River Junction, VT: Chelsea Green Publishing Company, 1996.

Elements of Style: A Practical Encyclopedia of Interior Architectural Details from 1485 to the Present. New York: Simon & Schuster, 1996. (Revised Edition, Stephen Calloway, Ed.)

Fradkin, Philip. *A River No More: The Colorado River and The West.* New York: Alfred A. Knopf, Inc., 1981.

Hirsch, Dena. *Union of Eagles-El Paso/Juarez.* El Paso, TX: Rainbow in a Tree Publications, Inc., 1987.

Hitchmough, Wendy. *The Arts & Crafts Lifestyle and Design.* Canada: Watson-Guptill Publications, 2000.

Hodoba, Theodore. *Growing Desert Plants: From Windowsill to Garden.* Santa Fe, NM: Red Crane Books, 1995.

Hunter, Linda Mason. *Southwest Style: A Home-Lover's Guide to Architecture and Design.* Flagstaff, AZ: Northland Publishing Company, 2000.

Iowa, Jerome. *Ageless Adobe: History and Preservation in Southwestern Architecture.* Santa Fe, NM: Sunstone Press, 1985.

Lamb, Susan. *Pueblo and Mission: Cultural Roots of the Southwest.* Flagstaff, AZ: Northland Publishing Company, 1997.

MacMahon, James A. *The Audubon Society Nature Guides: Deserts.* New York: Alfred A. Knopf, 1985.

Mather, Christine & Woods, Sharon. *Santa Fe Style.* New York: Rizzoli International Publications, Inc., 1986.

McAlester, Virginia & McAlester, Lee. *A Field Guide to America's Historic Neighborhoods and Museum House; The Western States.* New York: Alfred A. Knopf, 1998.

McGregor, Suzi Moore & Trulsson, Nora Burba. *Living Homes.* San Francisco: Chronicle Books, 2001.

Moore, Suzi. *Under the Sun.* Canada: Bullfinch Press, 1995.

Parachek, Ralph E. *Desert Architecture.* Phoenix, AZ: Parr of Arizona, 1967.

Romero, Orlando & Larkin, David. *Adobe: Building and Living with Earth.* New York: Houghton Mifflin Company, 1994.

Sanford, Trent Elwood. *The Architecture of the Southwest.* Tucson, AZ: The University of Arizona Press, 1950.

Seth, Sandra & Seth, Laurel. *Adobe! Homes and Interiors of Taos, Santa Fe and the Southwest.*

Stanford, CT: Architectural Book Publishing Company, 1988.

Sierra Club Guide to the National Parks of the Desert Southwest. New York: Stewart, Tabori & Chang, 1984.

Sunset Western Garden Book. Menlo Park, CA: Sunset Publishing Corporation, 2001. (7th Edition, Kathleen Norris Brenzel, Ed.)

Susanka, Sarah. *The Not So Big House.* Newtown, CT: The Taunton Press, Inc., 1998.

Wakely, David. *A Sense of Mission: Historic Churches of the Southwest.* San Francisco, CA: Chronicle Books, 1994.

Wallis, Michael. *Route 66: The Mother Road.* New York: St. Martin's Press, 1990.

Warren, Nancy Hunter. *New Mexico Style: A Sourcebook of Traditional Architectural Details.* Santa Fe, NM: Museum of New Mexico Press, 1986.

Webster, Dottie & Morris, Pamela. *A Window on Sedona.* Sedona, AZ: Cinnamon Stone Publishing, 2000.

Weinstein, Gayle. *Xeriscape Handbook: A How-To Guide to Natural, Resource-Wise Gardening.* Golden, CO: Fulcrum Publishing, 1999.

Desert USA
www.desertusa.com

National Park Service
www.nps.gov

Sustainable Building Sourcebook
www.greenbuilder.com

Index

Note: Italic page numbers indicate photographs.